Bound to be Beautiful

HERBERT PRESS
Bloomsbury Publishing Plc
50 Bedford Square, London, WC1B 3DP, UK
Bloomsbury Publishing Ireland Limited,
29 Earlsfort Terrace, Dublin 2, D02 AY28, Ireland

BLOOMSBURY, HERBERT PRESS and the Herbert Press
logo are trademarks of Bloomsbury Publishing Plc

First published in Great Britain in 2026

A catalogue record for this book is available from the British Library
Library of Congress Cataloguing-in-Publication data has been applied for

ISBN: 978-1-78994-238-5; eBook: 978-1-78994-241-5

2 4 6 8 10 9 7 5 3 1

Typeset in Quasimoda by Emilia Kalyvides
Printed and bound in China by RR Donnelley Asia Printing Solutions Ltd, Dongguan, Guangdong

To find out more about our authors and books visit
www.bloomsbury.com and sign up for our newsletters
For product safety related questions contact
productsafety@bloomsbury.com

Bari Zaki

Bound to be Beautiful

Over 20 Bookbinding Projects that Inspire and Delight

HERBERT PRESS
LONDON · OXFORD · NEW YORK · NEW DELHI · SYDNEY

CONTENTS

PREFACE

In my early twenties, I received an Italian blank book from a friend. He had made the first entry in it for me: an endearing doodle. I think of this as my first 'Dorothy' moment, when I found my way home to my earlier love of paper...

I grew up around paper; my dad was a printer, and he regularly brought home paper in various forms and formats: stacks, scraps, pads and assorted printed samples of paper. This was my absolute favourite part of the day. I squirrelled away every single piece and spent hours in my little walk-in closet arranging, rearranging and making little booklets. My technique at the time was stapling several sheets together and hand-lettering a title or doodle on the 'cover' page.

My other favourite papery moments were when I was visiting my dad at work. While he was on the phone, in meetings, or talking with clients, I would find my way to the back of the 'shop' – that was the term for where all the huge printing presses were humming and thumping away. The smell of ink, padding glue, the sound of bindery carts rolling across the hardwood flooring; it was all intoxicating. My brothers spent much of their time assisting the pressman and making deliveries. My dad reminisces fondly about how I spent much of my time combing the shelves for printed letterheads and envelopes, climbing up and into the scrap bins, amassing stacks of paper scraps for making books and assembling stationery sets for my friends.

Holding my new gifted Italian blank book in my hands made my heart pitter-patter. It reignited my love of paper and the idea of making books, no matter how basic. Several days later I wandered into Paper Source – then a small, independently owned stationery shop in Chicago – to see what I might discover. Inside a plexiglass cube, I spied a handmade book. I was mesmerized and intensely curious: somebody made this by hand? I decided right then and there that I needed to learn how to do that too!

I began by taking an eight-week workshop at Artist Book Works in Chicago. In the first session, we learned how to make a simple pamphlet book, and then we moved on to stitch a Japanese-style book. This was much more intricate and decorative. Eventually, we learned to make a case-bound book. I was enthralled and continued to make book after book after book.

I soon discovered Aiko's Art Materials, an enchanting shop specializing in Japanese papers, ceramics, books, fabrics and sumi-e supplies. It was the papers that spoke to me so intently, and soon it became my home away from home. I visited frequently and spent hours there, admiring and choosing papers. Sadly, they closed in 2008 after nearly 40 years in business. As a parting gift, the owner, Chuck Izui, gifted me one of their original card cabinets, which is now a prominent and beloved fixture at Bari Zaki Studio.

Paper is an enormous subject and yet the love we have for it can be as straightforward as being drawn to a pattern, liking the way it feels in our hands, how it folds and scores, or how it takes ink or watercolour. Each time I'm introduced to a new book-weight paper, my first inclination is to fold it into a signature. I encourage you to experiment and try out different papers that speak to you. Making books is all about paper and making something with the papers we love.

Additionally, I encourage you to enjoy using the books you make, to share them with your nearest and dearest, and to fill them with stories, drawings, doodles, musings, photos and ephemera. The pages we create are treasures, mementoes and time capsules. They are a joy to revisit, refer to, and to remind us of where we've been, how we've felt and, of course, to bring a smile to our paper-loving hearts.

INTRODUCTION

This is a how-to book about making hand-bound books that are beautiful to behold, as well as a joy to use. The projects are ideal for the bookbinding novice, or perhaps even a more experienced binder looking for inspiration. It outlines techniques and how to combine the ones the reader finds most satisfying.

The first chapter, **Tools, Materials and Techniques**, begins with an overview of the basic bookbinding tools and techniques used for each of the projects in the following chapters. I list each with a short description of how and when to use them, and this knowledge is hugely important to the outcome of a handmade book. You will be using them repeatedly, and once you become more comfortable with them (especially glueing) you'll be able to focus more on the steps for each project. I hope you find my suggestions helpful, but I encourage you to try things out and find the tools and techniques that suit you best.

The projects progress by skill level, and each chapter will introduce you to new techniques. You can start with any chapter that speaks to you, no matter your experience. Some of the basic techniques are repeated in each chapter; for example, you will be folding a full-sized sheet into signatures at the beginning of every project.

I have chosen specific materials for each of the projects, and I describe them and explain why they suit each structure. I realize that not all materials are available everywhere, so I have suggested alternatives when possible. You can find some alternative supplies in the **Resources** and **Glossary** sections at the back of the book.

At the end of the book, there is a small gallery of Bari Zaki Studio past projects, including photos of the same structure using different materials for additional inspiration.

The book structures I have chosen suit many different purposes, from drawing and collaging, to collecting ephemera and displaying photographs. I encourage you to use your books as when we begin to fill the pages, our books come alive.

I have made all these projects many, many times with a multitude of materials. Some are straightforward, others are more challenging. No matter what, the making of a book is incredibly satisfying, and I hear this from my students all the time. Even when a book is a bit wonky, it's still a happy moment.

Please use #boundtobebeautiful and tag @barizaki so that I can see the books you make! Wishing you many blissful bookbinding moments!

— **Bari Zaki**
Bari Zaki Studio

1

TOOLS, MATERIALS AND TECHNIQUES

TOOLS AND MATERIALS

Less is more when it comes to bookbinding tools. There's no need to invest hugely to make beautiful books, except maybe in paper. The tools listed in this chapter I consider the most basic and essential. As you begin to make more books, you will get a feel for what you enjoy working with, in terms of both materials and tools.

Paper ↓

One of the first things to consider when making a book is what weight of paper you will use for your pages. I've made books with paper as thin and lightweight as airmail (20–60 gsm) and as heavy as watercolour (300 gsm). They both present their joys and challenges but, depending on the binding style you are making, each folds and can be stitched beautifully. The two papers I use throughout the book are Hahnemühle Bugra (135 gsm) and Stonehenge (250 gsm) – both are 100% cotton. Together, these papers cover nearly every use from pen and ink, to watercolour, graphite and colour pencil.

Bone folder ↓

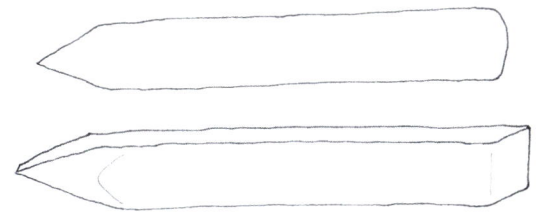

The bone folder is an essential bookbinding tool, available in an assortment of sizes. The one you will see most throughout the book measures 6 in/15.2 cm tall, has a pointed tip and gently rounded bottom. With this humble tool you can fold, score and burnish.

I highly recommend a Teflon bone folder when you are glueing. It has an incredibly smooth surface and simply glides over the paper or bookcloth you are burnishing. It will not mar, scratch or scrunch your paper.

Rulers ↓

You can make many books successfully with just a basic 12 in/30 cm metal ruler and a 30°/60° 10 in/25 cm triangle ruler. When working on larger projects, it's nice to have larger rulers, but it's not necessary. You can use them in tandem when working on larger books, like so:

· Trim or score to the tip of the triangle, place your metal ruler up against your triangle ruler, slide your triangle ruler along the metal ruler, set the metal ruler aside and finish scoring or trimming.

Shipping clerk's knife ↓

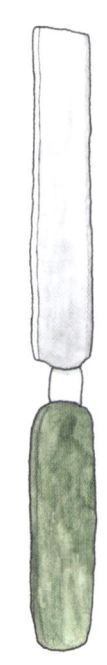

When paired with the bone folder, the shipping clerk's knife will help you create luscious, hand-torn edges on your signatures. It can be tricky to use at first, but I think you will come to love it. Here are my tips for using the knife:

· After you've made your first fold, hang the folded side slightly off the edge of the table. Place the knife between the fold, holding it on the diagonal, and slowly begin to pull the knife towards you. As you do this the knife will naturally begin to cut the paper. You might feel as though you'd like to push the knife forwards, but it's not necessary.
· If the knife goes askew, don't fret, just stop and take it slowly when you start again, using short strokes until you've cut the sheet in half, creating a lovely deckled edge. If you do cut off the edge of the sheet, your pages will have a slightly more exaggerated deckle, which – in my opinion – looks quite beguiling. Embrace the imperfections!

↑ I love the exaggerated deckled edges on the bottom book! I think it gives the book character and personality. This is my favourite photo to show students – whether they are making their first book, or have made many.

All about awls ↓

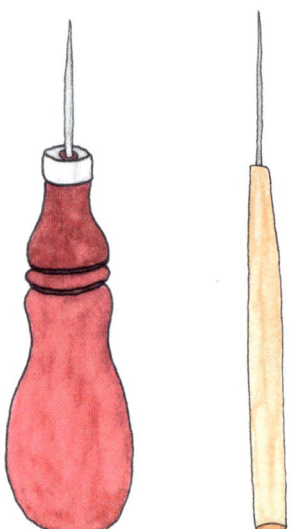

Awls are available in a variety of point sizes, gauges and handle shapes. The wooden handles feel good in your hand and are the nicest to use. These are the three I use most:

· The lightweight awl is perfect for piercing the sewing stations of your signatures. I haven't yet found any other uses for this size, probably because it is a little dainty, but I wouldn't use anything else for the job.
· The medium awl, with replaceable point, is great when making a Coptic-stitch or Japanese-style binding, and for when you need to create a spine template for a more detailed decorative spine stitching.
· The heavyweight awl has the thickest gauge (not shown). This is good to have on hand if you need to create larger holes in your Coptic-stitch hardcovers or the pages of a Japanese-style book. I also like to use this to get the holes started, then I come in with the medium awl to finish so that the holes look sleek and not too large.

Craft knife ↓

X-ACTO and Excel are the two knife brands I use most (#1 knife and #11 blades). If this is your first time using one of these knives I recommend testing with different styles and thicknesses of paper before you start your project. Here are my thoughts and tips for how best to use the knife:

· The best way to hold your knife is the way you hold a pen – gently, between your thumb and middle finger while resting your forefinger on the top for adjusting pressure. Use light to medium pressure; it will save your wrist and shoulders from tension, aches and pains, as well the tip of your blade.
· Go gently. You don't need to cut the paper or bookcloth in one go.
· I find that anchoring the ruler (or triangle ruler) with a little more pressure so that it doesn't shift or wiggle as you cut is more useful than pressing hard with the knife. You may need to run the blade over the area you are trimming more than once, but the slice itself will be smoother.

Glue brushes ↓

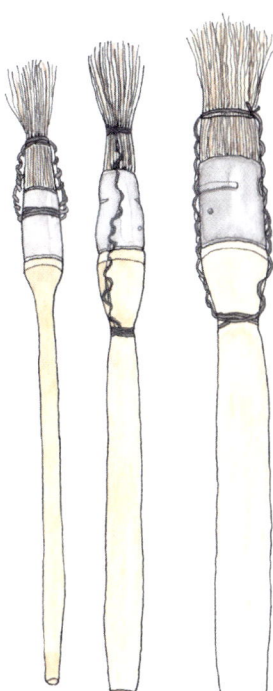

There are a handful of options when it comes to glue brushes, but my favourites come from the UK and have solid wooden handles and hog's hair bristles. I find that the stiffer the brush, the more control I have over the glue.

If you take good care of them, they will serve you well for years. I recommend rinsing them thoroughly in warm water as soon as you have finished glueing, then soaking the almost-clean bristles in fresh water overnight to prevent any glue residue hardening inside the bristle block. Gently squeeze out the excess water and rest the handle on the edge of your sink or upright in a cup, so that the bristles can breathe.

You will notice after using them only once that the bristles become stiffer once dry, and that's ok. Once you let the dried brush rest in your glue cup for a few minutes, the bristles begin to soften and you can glue with ease.

It is fine to leave the wire bridle on your brush – you will notice you have more control over the glue this way. If you do remove the wire, you will notice that the bristles splay and you will end up with more glue on your materials than you wish.

Cutting surfaces ↓

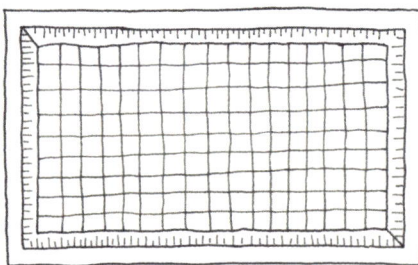

The best cutting surface is a self-healing mat. Most of these mats sport a grid pattern, which comes in handy for measuring on the spot. They are available in a wide range of sizes. Most art or office supply shops stock them. I've seen them in three different colours: black with a pale grey grid, green with a pale yellow grid, and frosty white with a black grid.

Book press for case binding ↓

There is only one style of book press you need for making a case-bound book. The book press in Chapter 10 (and above) is made from lightweight plywood, has a handle for ease of positioning the book and, most importantly, has two brass strips – top and bottom – that extend slightly from the plywood boards. Once you position your book in the press and tighten it in place, these brass strips actually 'crimp' your hinged cover while pressing.

Bookbinding needles ↓

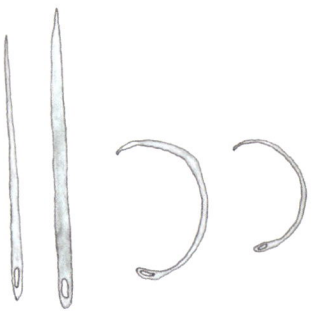

· The size 18 bookbinding needle is the ultimate basic, and I use it for almost everything. It's easy to thread with 4-ply Irish waxed thread and unwaxed linen thread. Size 25 is slightly thicker with a larger eye, and it neatly accommodates 7-ply thread.
· You will need a curved needle (2 × 21 mm) for any Coptic-stitch binding. It will accommodate both the 4-ply and 7-ply waxed thread. The slightly smaller size (2.5 × 20 mm) is definitely a bit daintier but it does not disappoint when you're stitching. 4-ply thread is best to use with this needle. There are numerous curved needle sizes to choose from and I recommend choosing the one that feels best in your hand.
· Embroidery needles are also nice to use for stitching, specifically the no. 18, because the gauge is similar to the size 18 bookbinding needle, but it has a slightly wider eye, so you could use it with the 7-ply waxed linen thread.

Hole punch ↓

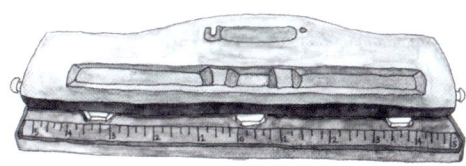

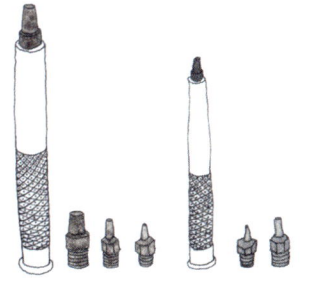

The three-hole punch is the perfect tool to use on a screw-post binder for the spine piece template and pages. I find that one with movable punches is the most useful, as you can arrange the holes where you need them to be, depending on the binder. If you only have a two-hole punch, that isn't a problem.

My single hole punch of choice is Tandy Leather's Leather Punch Set. It comes in two handy sizes, mini and maxi, and both come with six interchangeable punch sizes, from 0.08 to 0.32. I use the mini punch size (0.19 in/4.77 mm) when punching the holes for the screw-post binder spine piece (in Chapter 7) and the 0.09 in/2.32 mm when I need to create smaller holes to weave a ribbon or cording through a piece of bookboard. It easily punches through 0.98 bookboard or ½-inch stack of paper. I also keep a stash of the other sizes on hand, just in case.

Pencil ↓

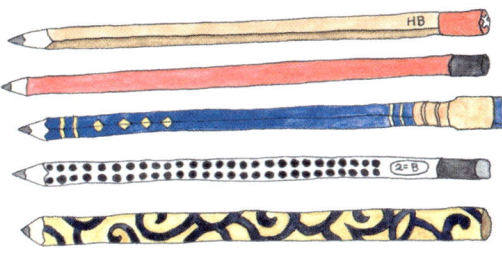

Pencils, oh pencils! One can never have enough. When making books and envelopes without a template, my recommendation is to use an HB as it's a happy medium in its utility. You will also need a white pencil for marking materials that have a darker backing. Whichever pencil you choose, be sure it's sharpened to a point so that the marks you make are precise. And, for the pleasure of aesthetics, decorating ubiquitous pencils will delight your work surface and bring joy to you and your projects (see Chapter 4).

Scissors ↓

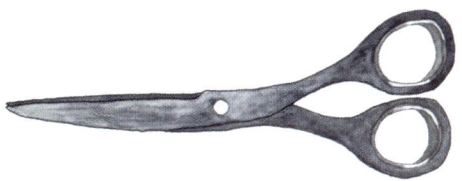

Scissors are available in a vast range of sizes and handle shapes including non-stick, left-handed and soft-grips, to name a few. My suggestion is that you find a pair that feels good in your hand. I use a small pair for trimming snippets of washi tape and thread and a large pair when making larger books.

Here's a list of adhesives that are nice to work with, non-toxic and acid free.

PVA glue

PVA is the most classic bookbinding adhesive. I've used it for as long as I've been making books (36 years!), and it is my go-to glue. It's water-based and fairly quick-drying.

Glue sticks

There are many glue sticks available and most are good. My favourites are Coccoina for its thick and creamy consistency (plus it smells like maraschino cherries). Yamato (see below) also comes in a stick and goes on more lightly and evenly. They are both good for collage work too.

Glue sticks are handy for sealing envelope flaps or adding a bit of extra adhesive when sealing your envelope/pocket flaps for softcover bindings. I love to use glue sticks because they are not water-based, so they are quick to dry and your papers will not pucker from moisture.

Adhesive tape

I absolutely love 3M's 415 double-sided transparent tape, primarily because it comes in a roll and is easily dispensed. It comes in four handy widths between ¼–1 in/0.5–2.5 cm. I love to use this tape when I'm sealing the envelope/pocket flaps for the softcover bindings – I rarely need to add additional glue. It's also great for when you're hand-folding an envelope from a heavier watercolour paper. You could use a glue stick, but using this tape is quicker.

It is good to have washi tape, painter's tape, or masking tape on hand. Washi tape is great for when you come to fill your book with photos, ephemera, swatches, or what-have-you.

Grafix Double Tack mounting sheets

These are very sticky and great when you're making a paper sandwich, as I like to call it, which you will discover when making your softcover bindings. I love using these sheets simply because they're quicker than glueing. Your cover will remain smooth and won't buckle or pucker.

In my experience these adhesive sheets are very sensitive to temperature and humidity. For example, in the drier winter months, when I peel back the first side it clings to the surface; this is good because you want the sheet to be very flat when attaching your backing sheet. In the summer months, when it's more humid, the sheet will begin to curl up, sometimes quickly. When this happens, use a bit of washi or masking tape to secure the very tips of each corner to the surface.

YES! paste

The consistency of this paste is extremely thick and not gooey in the least. I think of it as a giant glue stick in a tub, though to apply it you will need a standard glue brush. It's a great glue if you don't want your materials to buckle or pucker.

Yamato glue

This Japanese glue, which is made from tapioca starch, is a smooth, lightweight paste that comes in a squeezable tube. It dries s-l-o-w-l-y, giving you ample time to position and reposition whatever you are glueing. It behaves beautifully with a wide range of paper weights and textures, from thin, delicate tissuey papers to robust Chiyogami and Katazome. It can also attach bookcloth to bookboard, and it's perfect for collage work. You can use the glue directly from the tube, or add a droplet or two of water to thin the consistency.

 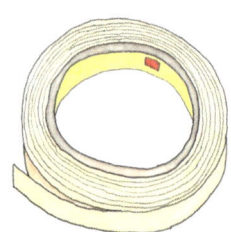 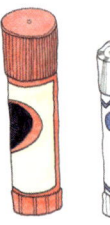 

TIPS AND TECHNIQUES

Here are several bookbinding techniques you will be repeating in the upcoming chapters. In nearly every project you will be using a bone folder and shipping clerk's knife to fold a parent sheet into a signature, or making a paper sandwich for your softcovers. As you repeat these steps they will become more natural to you and you'll begin to feel more confident as you continue to make more books.

Paper grain ↓

Paper grain is integral to how your book will open and function. In general, it is best to align the grain direction with the spine, although you'll discover that running the grain against the spine can be useful in certain projects. Here are some useful tips about paper grain:

· To determine the direction of the grain, take a single sheet and position it horizontally on your working surface. Gently roll the sheet in half, and use your hand to bounce the top of it a few times. Now roll the sheet lengthwise and bounce it again. If the bounce is less resistant when folded lengthwise, the grain is running the length of the paper, and vice versa.
· When you're folding a full-sized sheet down to a signature, your last fold will be with the grain.
· When you're stitching a non-adhesive binding, e.g., Coptic stitch, long stitch, or buttonhole

stitch, your grain doesn't need to run with the spine because you're not glueing the signatures in place. That said, when paper is folded against the grain, the fold is not as smooth.
· Scoring prior to folding can smooth out your folds. When I collaborated on a project to stitch 400 pamphlet-style bindings for a special edition, one of the books only had four pages (two sheets folded in half). We thought the book would benefit from having a bit more 'oomph', so in this case the pages were folded against the grain. The printer scored the sheets so that they'd fold more smoothly.
· When you're making a case-bound book, you are glueing up the spine before casing in your book block. In this case, the grain of your signatures should run with the spine, otherwise your pages will be wonky and your book will not open nicely.

Folding signatures ↓

Typically, a signature is four pieces of paper folded in half to make up an eight-page folio. However, it can vary depending on what best suits the paper you are folding and the book you are binding.

1. Position your paper horizontally on your working surface. Fold it in half gently, lining up the four corners. Anchor the sheet with one hand, take your bone folder in the other and fold the sheet in half by sliding your bone folder up to the top and back down to the bottom, creating a nice crisp fold.

2. Position your sheet with the fresh fold facing you and hang it slightly off the edge of the table. Place your shipping clerk's knife between the fold at a 45° angle, keep the knife parallel with the fold and slice it in half.

3. Use your bone folder to fold each of these sheets in half horizontally, one at a time, and slice again with your shipping clerk's knife.

Position your adhesive sheet horizontally and peel away one side. If it doesn't curl, great! You can skip ahead to the next step. If it does, take four small pieces of washi tape and use them to anchor the corners of the sheet to your surface at the very tips.

1. Take your backing paper and hold it up on one side while lining it up on the other short side. Once in place, press the edge of the sheet down onto the adhesive edge and then s-l-o-w-l-y begin to roll the paper onto the adhesive. Use your bone folder to smooth out any bumps or ridges.

Note → Don't fret if it's not perfectly aligned – you will be squaring off all four edges when you finish making the paper sandwich. Likewise, if you have any bubbles or creases, don't worry! I find that burnishing them with a bone folder will smooth them out easily.

2. Flip the sheet over and expose the adhesive on the other side.

Repeat Steps 1 and 2 with your decorative paper. You won't need any tape for this step because the weight and thickness of the backing paper will help keep your cover flat on the surface.

3. Next, you will square off all four sides of your paper sandwich by trimming away about ⅛ in/3 mm all around (or a smidgen more if needed). Place your cover decorative side up. Take your triangle ruler and line it up at the bottom edge, leaving about ⅛ in/3 mm exposed to the right of the ruler. Use your craft knife and carefully slice away the first short end. Rotate your sheet 90° so that the freshly trimmed side is facing you, position the triangle ruler on the long edge and trim. Repeat on the other two sides.

Covering button knots with paper scraps ↓

1. Take a scrap of paper for each button and trim them to 1 × 1 in/2.5 × 2.5 cm, or larger – it's your choice! You can use a craft knife or scalloped/pinking shears.

2. Use either a glue stick or double-adhesive tape to attach it over the knot at the back of the button. Place the envelope (or cover) button-side up and press.

Keeping your signatures in order ↓

Place your stack of signatures in front of you with the folds facing you. Each time you remove a signature to pierce the sewing stations, place it down with the fold of the signature facing away from you. You can also number them in light pencil in the upper right corner, and pencil a light 'X' on the front cover. This will help you keep everything in order.

A note about scoring ↓

When you're making two opposite score lines, and measuring the second, remember to place your ruler a smidgen to the left of the existing score line to achieve a more accurate measurement.

If you place the triangle ruler directly over the pencil marks, the distance between your score lines will be shortened.

Stitching techniques ↓

· You can use one length of thread to stitch your entire book, though if this is your first time stitching then I would recommend that you divide your thread in two. If the thread is too long it often gets tangled up and makes for a less pleasant stitching experience. When you divide your thread, you will add the second half by way of a weaver's knot (seen in Chapter 8), or you can even tie a double knot. It is best to add this at one of the middle stations.

· Keep an eye on the tension of your stitches as you work – it isn't easy to tighten them once they're in place – and tighten in the direction you are working in. Don't pull the stitch towards you as you will tear your signature!

· To keep your book block nicely squared throughout the stitching process, continuously jog your spine and bottom of the book after stitching in each signature.

· When you 'enter' a sewing station, you bring your needle into the book from the outside. When you 'exit' a station, you leave the book and finish with your needle outside.

Weaver's knot ↓

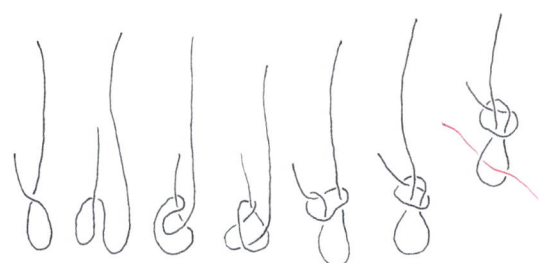

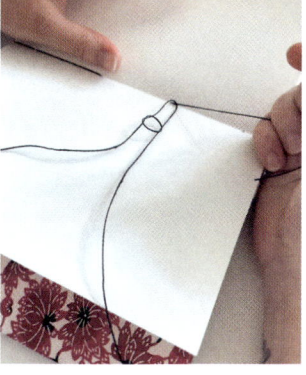
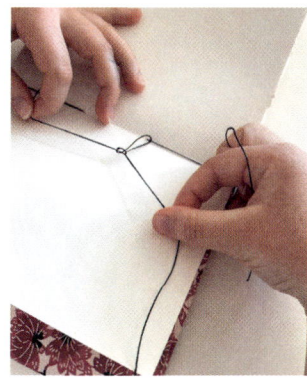

1. Hold a 5 in/12.5 cm tail of thread over your forefinger and wrap it around to the top creating a loop.

2. Pull the loop off your finger, and use your thumb and forefinger to go through the loop, grab the thread on the other side of the loop, pull it forward through the loop till it looks like a noose.

3. Take your needle, come through the top of the noose, bring it as close to the sewing station as you can, then pull tightly on both tail ends

of the noose so that it secures around the original thread.

4. Snip the two tails and thread your needle with the new thread and carry on stitching.

Note → When you tighten the new piece of thread around the old, you can often feel it snap in place (which is very satisfying) it feels like the knot is 'locked in'. That said, quite often it doesn't do that when using a waxed thread.

2

ELEGANT ENVELOPMENTS

BUTTONED-UP ELEGANT ENVELOPE BOOKLET

A charming ensemble featuring a pair of interior envelope-pockets on the inside of the covers and a sturdy centre envelope stitched into a single signature. Two string-and-button closures hold it all together in an exquisite receptacle for ephemera or treasured memories. The finished booklet measures 5½ × 7½ × ¼ in/14 × 19 × 0.5 cm, and the presentation envelope measures 6¾ × 8½ × ¼ in/17 × 21.5 × 0.5 cm.

Materials ↓

- · 2 sheets (matching or complementary) of Atelier Ecluse handmade 320 gsm papers (11 × 15 in/27.9 × 38.1 cm)
- · 1 sheet of Stonehenge 250 gsm paper (22 × 30 in/55.9 × 76.2 cm)
- · 3 lengths of 4-ply waxed linen thread in different colours (12 in/30.5 cm each)
- · 4 cheerful buttons (small-ish (½ in/1.3 cm) and medium-ish (¾ in/1.9 cm))

Tools ↓

- · bone folder
- · shipping clerk's knife
- · craft knife
- · metal ruler
- · 30°/60° triangle ruler (12 in/30.5 cm and 6 in/15.2 cm)
- · lightweight awl
- · size 18 bookbinding needle
- · glue stick
- · double-adhesive tape
- · pencil
- · scissors
- · cutting mat

Fold the signature ↓

Follow Steps 1–3 of **Folding signatures** (see **Techniques**, p.20). You now have four sheets, each measuring 11 × 15 in/27.9 × 38.1 cm [A+B].

Take one of your four pieces, fold it in half, slice again with your shipping clerk's knife, then take the two freshly cut sheets and use your working surface to line up the bottom edges. Use your bone folder to fold them in half, then set aside.

Hand-fold the inner envelope and attach the buttons ↓

1. Position one sheet of Stonehenge (11 × 15 in/279 × 381 mm) horizontally.

2. Take your ruler and measure 4 in/102 mm from the right edge (which will be your bottom flap). Line up your triangle ruler at the 4 in/102 mm mark and use your bone folder to score the sheet. Fold it over at the score and crease with your bone folder, then open and press flat [C].

3. Measure the width of your signature and make a note of it. Using your ruler and triangle ruler, measure up from your first score line to that measurement and score again using your bone folder to create the body of your envelope. Decide if you'd like your top flap to be deep or shallow, then trim accordingly. You will need an overlap of at least 1 in/25 mm [D+E].

4. Now position your sheet vertically. Use your ruler and triangle ruler to measure 1 in/25 mm from the right edge. Measure at both the top

and bottom of the sheet to ensure that your side flap will be even, then score with your bone folder. Fold over at the score line and burnish with your bone folder [F].

5. Measure the height of your signature. You will use this measurement to finish making the body of your envelope. Use your ruler and triangle ruler in tandem to measure the distance between your first side score line and what will be your second. Measure your sheet at the top and bottom to ensure the space between score lines is even, then score with your bone folder. Fold over and burnish as before [G].

6. Using a craft knife, trim the left flap to 1 in/25 mm to match the flap on the other side [H].

A ↓

B ↓

C ↓

D ↓

E ↓   **F** ↓   **G** ↓   **H** ↓

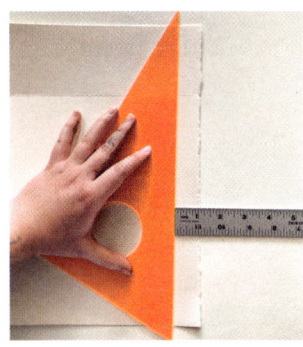  

Trim your envelope corners ↓

Note → You can pencil these trimming directions directly onto your sheet of Stonehenge. In my workshops I often suggest that students make up a template from cartridge paper for practice.

Note → Keep your corners! You will use these to make paper patches for the back of your envelope flaps [C].

1. Beginning at the bottom right corner, make a pencil mark ⅛ in/6 mm to the left of the score line. From the bottom left corner, make a pencil mark ⅛ in/6 mm to the right of the score line. Rotate your paper clockwise 90° and make a pencil mark ⅛ in/6 mm to the right of the score line, then ½ in/13 mm to the left of the next score line (for your side flap). Repeat these marks as you make your way around the sheet [A].

2. Starting again at the bottom right corner, place the tip of your pencil in the intersection of the score lines, then place your triangle ruler up against your pencil, line it up with the pencil mark at the edge of your sheet and draw a line. Repeat this step around the sheet.

3. Next you will slice away the corners at the pencil marks. Essentially, you're repeating the steps you just penciled in with your craft knife [B].

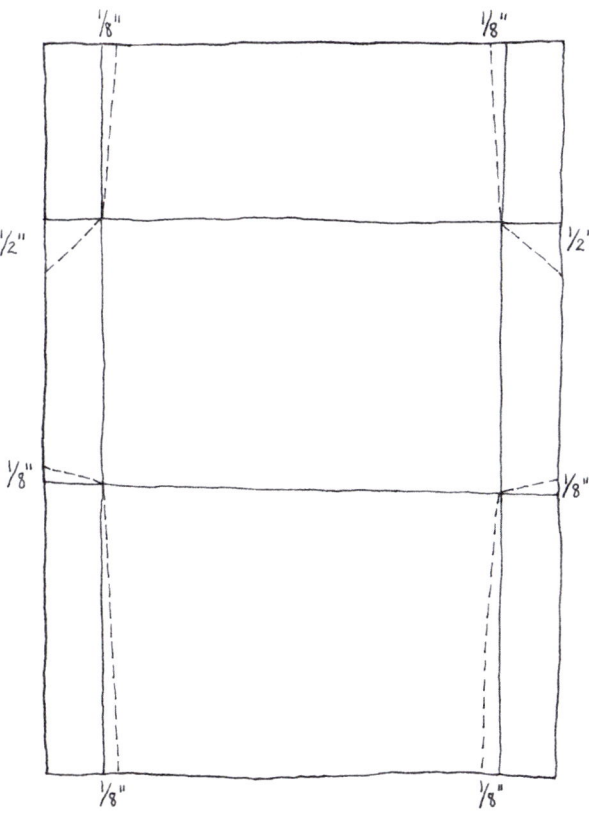

Attach buttons to the interior envelope and prepare the envelope for stitching ↓

1. Place one button on the top flap and one on the bottom flap in the position you'd like them to be. (There is no 'correct' measurement, this is purely personal preference.) Once they are in place, take your metal ruler and measure on each side to confirm that they are evenly placed. Take a freshly sharpened pencil and make a dot through the two buttonholes onto your envelope flaps. Then take your lightweight awl and pierce through the pencil marks [D].

2. Measure off two pieces of waxed linen thread 6 in/15 cm each. Thread through each of the buttons from the top and attach them through the top and bottom flaps of your envelope. Secure with a double knot (see Note) [E].

   Threading tip → If you struggle threading your thread through the pierced holes, squeeze the tip between your thumb and forefinger to stiffen the end, and if that doesn't work then take off a short snip with your scissors to give you a fresh end.

   Note → You want a little bit of breathing room behind the buttons to accommodate the closing string, because if you tie too tight, you risk tearing through the paper. Tie off each button with a taut (but not too tight) double knot at the back of the flaps. If the knot bulges, which it may very well do, use your bone folder to press it as flat as it will go.

A ↓

B ↓

C ↓

D ↓

E ↓

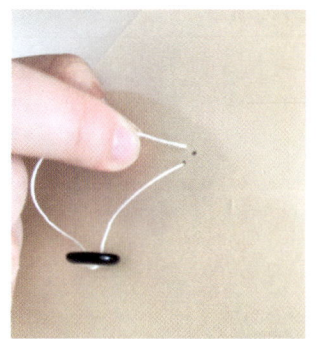

F ↓

G ↓

H ↓

Attach a paper patch behind the buttons ↓

Follow Steps 1–2 of **Covering button knots** (see **Techniques**, p.22), using the trimmed corners of your Stonehenge [F+G].

Trim two pieces of double-adhesive tape to the height of your bottom flap. If you prefer to use a glue stick, skip this step and apply the glue in the same area once you've finished stitching your booklet and hand-folding your presentation envelope [H].

You will seal your envelopes after you've finished stitching.

Prepare the cover with two interior envelopes/pockets ↓

1. Position your sheet of Atelier Ecluse paper horizontally and fold the sheet in half. Open the sheet and flatten. You've created your first score line, which forms the spine of the booklet.

2. Next, you will measure, score and fold your cover so that it wraps around your signatures nicely. When making a book, you typically work from the inside out, so here you begin with the spine measurement and work out from there. You will make a total of four additional score lines and folds that, when completed, will envelop your signature and the envelope inside your cover. You always want your score lines to be precise, but it's the second of the two corresponding score lines that requires the most precision.

3. Your next two score lines are the top and bottom folds of your cover. Position your cover vertically. Take one signature and place it at the spine score [A].

4. Nestle your single signature inside the spine and hold the cover up against the signature. Be sure that your signature is flush with the fold. As you hold the signature in place, let the cover fall flat to the surface. Take the long end of your triangle ruler, place it up against the signature at the left, move the signature aside, then use the tip of your bone folder to score all the way from top to bottom. Fold over at the crease, burnish with your bone folder then open the cover up and flatten [B].

5. Measure the height of your signature. Then rotate your cover 180° so it's vertical. Nestle your signature into the spine score, and the recent side score. I always repeat this step so that I'm confident the signature is perfectly squared against each score line before I proceed.

A ↓

B ↓

C ↓

D ↓

6. Place your triangle ruler on the opposite side of the signature (this step is helpful to get your triangle ruler in place). Move the signature aside and keep your triangle ruler anchored in position, take your metal ruler and scooch the triangle ruler over 1/16 in/1.5 mm to compensate for the score line. Do this at the top and again at the bottom to be sure the distance is perfectly even [C].

Tip → Make a pencil mark at the top and bottom where you've already measured just in case your triangle ruler shifts. You can then reposition it easily, just to the left of the pencil marks.

7. Use your bone folder to score all the way up and down. Fold over at the crease, burnish with your bone folder, open your cover and press it flat again.

8. Your next two score lines will be your fore-edge. This measurement does not have to be as precise as the previous ones, as I think it's nice to have a little extra room here.

Note → Having a little extra room at the fore-edge is helpful because once you close the cover of your book, the signature naturally pushes forward a bit. If you didn't add a bit extra, the signatures might protrude from your cover.

9. Measure the width of your signature, then add 1/4 in/6 mm to that measurement. Position your cover horizontally and place your triangle ruler to the left of the spine score (for reference, my measurement is 5⅞ in/149 mm). Now use your ruler to confirm the distance is even at the top and bottom. Repeat the measure, pencil mark and scoring instruction on the other side. Then use the tip of your bone folder to

score from top to bottom. Fold it over on the score line, burnish with your bone folder, then open the cover flat, rotate your cover 180° and repeat on the other side [D].

10. Now you will mark the cover where you will trim the corners so that your flaps will taper in nicely. Position your cover horizontally, as in the illustration. Make little pencil marks, beginning at the bottom right corner and working your way clockwise.

11. At the bottom right corner make a pencil mark 1/4 in/6 mm to the left of your vertical score line.

12. Make pencil marks 1 in/25 mm to the right of the spine score, and another mark 1 in/25 mm to the left of the spine score.

13. Making your way to the left corner, make a pencil mark 1/4 in/6 mm to the right of your vertical score line.

14. Rotate your cover 90° and make a pencil mark 1/4 in/6 mm to the left of that score line.

Continue making your way around the cover until you have marked all four corners and the spine.

15. Reposition your cover horizontally. Place your triangle ruler at the intersection of the score lines and place the tip of your craft knife into the intersection. Line your triangle ruler up with the pencil mark at the bottom edge of your cover, then slice. Make your way around the cover, repeating this action on all your corners and spine.

Construct your cover ↓

1. Place strips of double-adhesive tape on the side flaps as shown [A].

2. Separate one of your signatures into two and trim both pieces to 7¼ × 5¼ in/184 × 133 mm. Place a strip of double-adhesive tape to both folded pieces ⅛ in/1.6 mm from the folded edge [B+C].

3. Expose the adhesive strip on both of your trimmed signatures and place one trimmed signature adhesive side down ⅛ in/1.6 mm away from the spine score and centred from top and bottom. Repeat on the opposite cover [D].

4. Now expose the adhesive strips on your side flaps. Place the top and bottom flaps down first, then place your side flap over and press. Repeat on the other side. Press the cover under a heavy weight for about 10 minutes [E].

Note → If you're using a glue stick to secure your flaps you will want to press the cover longer.

A ↓

B ↓

C ↓

D ↓

E ↓

Prepare your booklet for stitching ↓

1. Place your cover, flat on the surface with the spine fold facing you. The signature does not need to be inside. Place your metal ruler flat on the surface so it's running along the spine.

2. Make one pencil mark in the centre on the fold of the spine. Then make another pencil mark 2 in/51 mm above and below the centre [A].

3. Place your envelope inside your signature and your signature inside the cover [B].

4. Take your lightweight awl and pierce through the cover and the signature with its envelope. There are a lot of layers of paper and it can be a bit challenging to pierce through. Go slowly, be gentle and be sure your fingers are nowhere near the interior fold [C].

A ↓

B ↓

C ↓

Stitch your booklet ↓

You can begin stitching on the inside or the outside of the book. If you start on the inside, your thread tails will end up on the inside and vice versa. I prefer to have the tails on the outside because you can embellish the thread with a couple of seed beads (without forgetting to tie a knot, of course!). Either way, the stitch is the same [A+B].

1. Enter the centre sewing station [C].

2. Go up to the top station and exit the booklet [D].

3. Go down to the bottom station and enter the booklet.

4. Exit the centre station.

5. Tighten and tie off with a double knot [E].

A ↓

B ↓

C ↓

D ↓

6. When the tails are on the outside of the cover, they will look nice when you tie a half knot on each tail about 2 in/51 mm from the centre, then snip them ¼ in/6 mm after the knot.

7. Finish off by sealing the flaps to your inner envelope [F].

Note → Because there are several layers of paper to stitch through, it can be challenging to push the needle through all the layers together perfectly, and you can sometimes unintentionally pierce a second hole through the cover. To avoid this, first come through the envelope (if starting on the inside), then the signature and then the cover. Once you do this, the two other stations should line up more easily. If they don't, repeat this process from the outside in.

E ↓

F ↓

Hand-fold your outer/presentation envelope ↓

You will make your outer/presentation envelope in almost exactly the way you made your inner envelope, with just a few adjustments to accommodate the thickness of your booklet.

Note → When making your outer envelope, keep your scraps for using as patches for the button backing.

1. Position your second piece of Atelier Ecluse paper horizontally on your working surface and place your triangle ruler 4 in/102 mm up from the right edge of your cover. Take your bone folder and score along your triangle ruler. Fold over your cover at the crease, then open and flatten [A].

A ↓

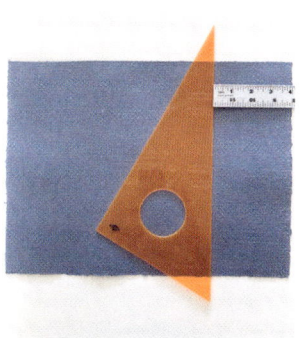

B ↓

C ↓

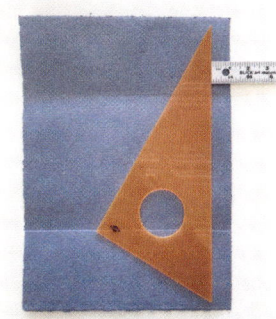

D ↓

2. Measure the width of your booklet and add ¾ in/19 mm (this extra measurement accommodates for puffiness of your booklet). Position your triangle ruler up from the first score line, measure at the top and bottom to be sure the distance between the score line and triangle ruler is even (6⅞ in/175 mm). Use your bone folder to score along your triangle ruler [B].

3. Position your cover vertically. Measure 1 in/25 mm in from the right edge at the top and bottom. Use your bone folder to score along your triangle ruler. Fold over at the score line, burnish with your bone folder, then open and flatten [C].

4. Measure the height of your booklet and add 1 in/25 mm [D].

5. Position your triangle ruler to the right of the first side score line at the top and bottom, and use your bone folder to score along the triangle ruler. Fold over at the score line, burnish with your bone folder or palm of your hand, then open and flatten.

Finish your outer envelope ↓

1. Trim your envelope corners and attach your buttons exactly as you did with the inner envelopes (on p.31) [A].

2. Add a strip of adhesive to your bottom envelope flap. Seal and press [B].

A ↓

B ↓

Add the closing string ↓

Measure a length of thread that will wind around both buttons a couple of times, plus a few extra inches for tying on. Wrap the thread around either button, as you prefer. Tie a double knot, gently. I like to press the button to squish the bulkiness of the thread knot.

Happiness ensues!

STRING-AND-BUTTON ENVELOPE CASE

One incredibly deluxe envelope case with a string-and-button closure. For the finale, you will cover a binder's half-dozen teeny butterfly clips in Japanese Chiyogami paper.

Materials ↓

- 1 sheet of St-Armand handmade 320 gsm paper
  (11 × 14 in/279 × 356 mm)
- 8 Carta Pura notecards (A6) and envelopes (C6)
- 2 beautiful buttons (¾ in/1.9 cm)
- 1 length of waxed linen thread in a complementary colour
  (10 in/25.5 cm)
- 7 tiny butterfly clips
- 1 sheet of Chiyogami 70 gsm paper

Alternative papers

- 1 sheet of 250 gsm watercolour paper (11 × 14 in/279 × 356 mm)
- 1 sheet of cover or card stock (80 or 100 lb/10 or 12 pt)
- A6 notecards or C6 envelopes (4 × 6 in/101 × 152 mm)

Tools ↓

- bone folder
- shipping clerk's knife
- craft knife
- metal ruler
- triangle ruler
- lightweight awl
- glue stick
- double-adhesive tape
- scissors
- cutting mat

Fold the envelope case ↓

1. Position your handmade paper horizontally. Measure 3½ in/89 mm from the right edge and score with the tip of your bone folder. Fold over and crease with your bone folder, then open and press flat [A].

> Note → Each time you score your sheet, fold it over and crease with your bone folder, then open it up and press flat. This accentuates the score line, making it easier to see and measure against your following score lines. I have drawn a pencil line inside my score lines so that you can see them more clearly.

2. Measure 1 in/25 mm to the left of your first score line, and score with your bone folder. This is your bottom/base spine.

3. Measure 4½ in/117 mm to the left of the second score line and score with your bone folder. This is the back body [B].

4. Measure 1¹⁄₁₆ in/27 mm to the left of the third score line and score with your bone folder. This is the top spine [C].

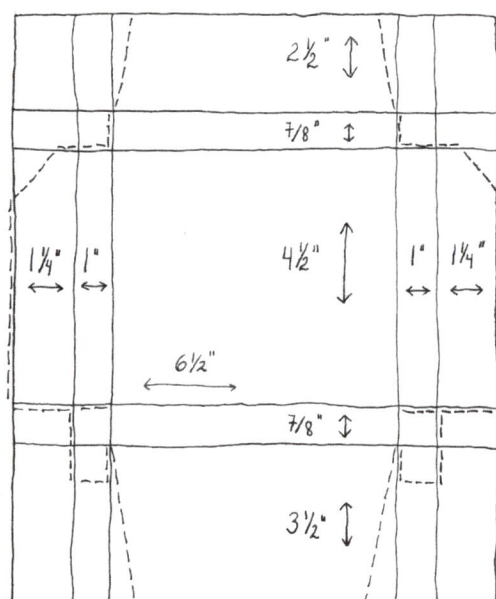

A ↓

B ↓

C ↓

D ↓

E ↓

F ↓

G ↓

> Note → You will have a bit of extra flap once you've finished scoring and folding these score lines. This is when you get to decide how deep you'd like your envelope flap and how it will suit your buttons.

5. Fold over the front flap and place your buttons where you'd like them to be, then measure (the flap pictured is 2¼ in/57 mm). You can use your craft knife to trim the flap to the suitable depth, or you can score with your bone folder and trim with your shipping clerk's knife, which will create a hand-torn deckled edge [D].

6. Position your paper vertically and place your envelope stack in the centre. Place your triangle ruler up against the left of your envelope stack, then set the stack aside. Measure the distance from the ruler to the right edge of the paper, at the top and bottom

(approximately 8¾ in/222 mm). Score with the tip of your bone folder [E].

7. Rotate your paper 180° so your score line is on the right. Measure the width of your envelope stack and add ⅛ in/3 mm (for a total width of 6½ in/165 mm). Use your ruler and triangle ruler in tandem and measure that distance to the left of your previous score line. Use the tip of your bone folder and score [F].

8. Now measure the thickness of your envelope stack. Position your paper vertically and measure (that thickness) to the left of the first vertical score line, score and then fold and crease. Repeat on the opposite side [G].

9. Now you will trim the corners. I've provided a lovely illustration for you to follow (see opposite).

Attach the buttons ↓

> Tip → If you struggle to thread the pierced holes, squeeze the tip of the thread between your thumb and forefinger to stiffen the end. If that doesn't work, snip the end with your scissors to freshen it up.

> Note → Don't forget to leave a bit of breathing room behind the buttons.

1. Place one button on the top flap and one on the bottom flap in your preferred position. Once they are spaced to your liking, take your metal ruler and measure either side to confirm that they are evenly placed.

2. Take a freshly sharpened pencil and make a pencil dot through the two buttonholes onto your envelope flaps [A].

A ↓

B ↓

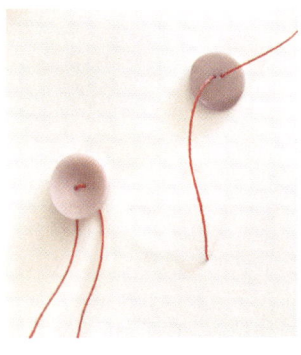

3. Take your lightweight awl and pierce through the pencil marks.

4. Measure off two 6 in/15 cm pieces of waxed linen thread. Thread through each of the buttons from the top and attach them through the top and bottom flaps of your envelope [B].

Follow Steps 1–2 from **Covering button knots** (see **Techniques**, p.22), using the trimmed corners of your envelope [A+B].

1. Trim four pieces of double-adhesive tape: two that are slightly shorter than your bottom flap; two that will fit on the small flaps.

2. Flip your envelope case over so that the exterior is facing up. Now attach the tape as shown in [C].

3. First expose the adhesive on the two small flaps. Then bring in your side flaps and seal those together [D].

4. Expose the strips of adhesive on the side flaps and bring up your top flap. Press and seal [E].

5. Take your length of waxed linen thread and tie a half knot around the top button, pull taut and then snip off the tail end. Wind the thread around the bottom and top buttons a few times then trim the thread to your liking [F].

A ↓

B ↓

C ↓

D ↓

E ↓

F ↓

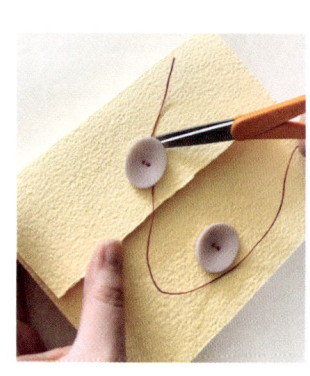

Cover butterfly clips ↓

When I cover butterfly clips in decorative paper, I typically make a bowlful for the shop, and so need to be efficient in my trimming process. I find it helpful to start with a letter-sized sheet, which I slice into long vertical pieces. I then cut them again horizontally. Whether you are making a small handful or a bowlful, the process is the same.

1. Position your decorative sheet vertically. Line a butterfly clip up against the right edge of the sheet and place your triangle ruler or metal ruler up against the clip on the left [A].

2. Slide the clip all the way up and down the sheet, confirming that the edge of the clip is perfectly aligned on the edge of the sheet.

3. Keep your ruler in place and use your craft knife to trim along the ruler's edge [B].

4. Lift the strip of paper and nestle the short edge up against the curl of the clip [C].

5. Wrap the paper around to the opposite nook and crease the paper in the curl of the clip.

6. Place the strip of decorative paper flat on the surface and use your ruler (or triangle ruler) and trim on the crease with your craft knife.

7. Before trimming the rest of your papers, wrap the measured piece around the clip to confirm it's not too short or too long, and make any adjustments if needed.

8. Position your template piece up against the longer strip and then slice additional pieces with your craft knife. Alternatively, you can measure the trimmed piece and use your ruler to measure the additional pieces.

9. Now take one of the trimmed papers, a piece of scrap paper and deploy your glue stick. Place the paper decorative side down and swish a bit of glue on the back [D].

A ↓

B ↓

C ↓

D ↓

E ↓

F ↓

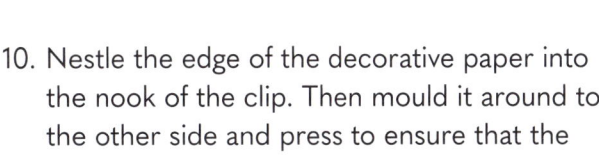

10. Nestle the edge of the decorative paper into the nook of the clip. Then mould it around to the other side and press to ensure that the paper has attached smoothly [E+F].

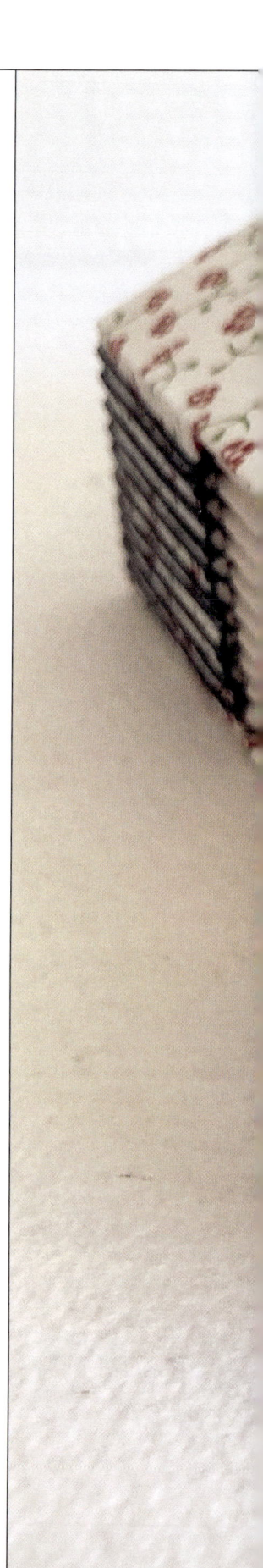

3

BUTTONHOLE-STITCH BINDING

WHAT YOU'LL MAKE

This binding style makes a wonderful sketchbook, photo album or journal. The little window on the spine provides endless visual delight, especially if you alternate or graduate the colours of the signatures within. Both front and back inside covers have an envelope/pocket. The final book measures approximately 5⅞ × 7½ × 1¼ in/149 × 190 × 32 mm.

Materials ↓

- 1 sheet of Rossi 85 gsm decorative paper (11 × 18 in/279 × 457 mm)
- 1 sheet of Grafix Double Tack (11 × 18 in/279 × 457 mm)
- 4 sheets of Stonehenge 250 gsm paper
    - 1 cover sheet (11 × 18 in/279 × 457 mm)
    - 3 page sheets (22 × 30 in/559 × 762 mm)
- 4-ply waxed linen thread (at least 5 yd/4.5 m)

Tools ↓

- bone folder
- shipping clerk's knife
- craft knife
- metal ruler
- triangle ruler
  (two sizes if possible)
- lightweight awl
- size 18 bookbinder's
  needle
- glue stick
- washi tape
- double-adhesive tape
- pencil
- scissors
- cutting mat

Fold the signatures ↓

One sheet of Stonehenge paper will yield four 4-page signatures (eight serendipitous sides). To make this buttonhole-stitch book, you will fold down three full-sized sheets to make 12 signatures. You will use ten for your pages, one for reinforcing your cover and one extra, which you can use for another book, or for experimenting.

Follow Steps 1–3 of **Folding signatures** (see **Techniques**, p.20). You now have four pieces, each measuring 11 × 15 in/217 × 381 mm [A–C].

1. Use your bone folder to fold each of these pieces in half, one at a time, and slice again [D].

2. Take the two freshly cut pieces and use your working surface to line up the bottom edges. Use your bone folder to fold them in half, then set aside. Carry on folding till you have a total of 12 4-page signatures [E+F].

> Note → There's no need to press your signatures after folding. The puffier the signatures, the more room there will be for adding collage, photos or bits of ephemera.

Make the paper sandwich for the cover ↓

Follow Steps 1–3 of **Making a paper sandwich** (see **Techniques**, p.21), using your Stonehenge cover sheet and Rossi decorative paper (11 × 18 in/279 × 457 mm) [G].

> Note → Next you will measure, score and fold your cover so that it wraps around your signatures nicely. When making a book, you are typically working from the inside out, so here you will begin with the spine measurement and work out from there. You will make a total of six score lines and folds. You always want to score precisely, but it's the second of the two corresponding score lines that requires the most precision.

A ↓

B ↓

C ↓

D ↓

E ↓

F ↓

G ↓

Score and fold the cover ↓

1. Position your freshly made cover horizontally, decorative side down, and measure the width. Halve that measurement and make a pencil mark there at the bottom of the cover [A].

2. Place your ten signatures flat on the surface and place your metal ruler vertically against the folds. Measure the thickness of your pages by gently compressing your signatures and releasing them; as you 'bounce' the signatures, you will find a happy medium between when the signatures are completely compressed and when you let them puff up a bit [B+C].

3. Halve your spine measurement and make a second pencil mark to the right of the centre pencil mark. This is where you will make your first spine score.

4. Position your triangle ruler flush with the bottom of the cover and use the tip of your bone folder to score all the way from top to bottom. Give it a good crease – you're scoring through three layers. Fold the cover over on this first score line, burnish with your bone folder, then open your cover flat [D].

5. For the second spine score (see **Techniques**, p.22, for my scoring tips) position your triangle ruler to the left of the first spine score line, plus a smidgen. Measure at the top and bottom of your cover to be sure the triangle ruler is positioned evenly, then use your bone folder to score the second spine score line. Fold at the crease and burnish with your bone folder, then open your cover flat.

6. The next score lines are the top and bottom folds of your cover. Position your cover vertically. Take one signature and place it at the spine score closest to you [E].

A ↓

B ↓

C ↓

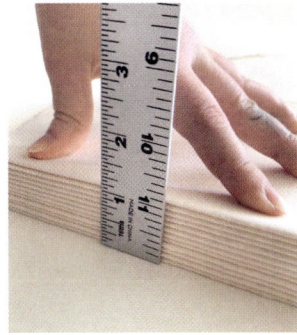

D ↓

E ↓

F ↓

G ↓

H ↓

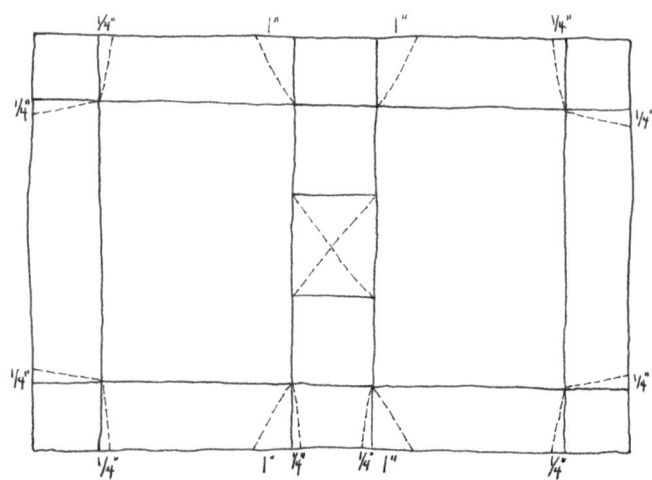

7. Hold the cover and spine up against the signature and be sure that your signature is flush with the fold. As you hold the signature in place, let the cover fall flat to the surface. Then take the long end of your triangle ruler, place it up against the signature at the left, move the signature aside, then use the tip of your bone folder to score all the way from top to bottom. Fold over at the score line, burnish with your bone folder, then open the cover up and flatten [F].

Note → If your triangle ruler is shorter than the width of the cover, use your metal ruler in tandem with your triangle ruler to extend your scoring line ability more easily [G].

8. Measure the height of your signature and then rotate your cover 180° so it's vertical again. Nestle your signature into the spine score and the side score, then place your triangle ruler up against the signature on the opposite side (this step is helpful to get your triangle ruler in place). Move the signature aside and add a smidgen to the measurement from the triangle ruler to what will be your score line. Use your bone folder to score all the way up and down. Fold over at the crease, burnish with your bone folder and open your cover flat again [H].

9. Your next two score lines will be the fore-edge. I like to add ¼ in/6 mm extra to the width of the book so that the signatures don't protrude from the cover. Measure the width of your signature, then add ¼ in/6 mm (or ⅛ in/3 mm if you prefer to have the width of your cover more flush with your fore-edge). Position your cover horizontally and place your triangle ruler 5⅞ in/149 mm (or 5¾ in/146 mm) to the left of the spine score at the left. Now use your ruler to confirm the distance is even at the top and bottom. Measure, mark and score as you did before, then use the tip of your bone folder to score from top to bottom. Fold on the score

line, burnish with your bone folder, then open the cover flat. Rotate your cover 180° and repeat on the other side [I].

Note → At this point, you can trim the side flaps to match your top and bottom flaps. You could also do this after you've trimmed your corners and created your window.

10. Now you will mark the cover where you will trim the corners so that your flaps will taper in nicely. Position your cover horizontally. Begin at the bottom right corner and work your way clockwise, making pencil marks to guide where you will trim your corners.

11. At the bottom right corner make a pencil mark ¼ in/6 mm to the left of your vertical score line [J].

12. Moving clockwise, make a pencil mark 1 in/25 mm to the right of the first spine score.

13. Make a pencil mark ¼ in/6 mm to the left of that spine score and the same mark to the right of the next spine score, and a pencil mark 1 in/25 mm to the left of that spine score.

14. Making your way to the left corner, make a pencil mark ¼ in/6 mm to the right of your vertical score line.

15. Rotate your cover 90° and make a pencil mark ¼ in/6 mm to the left of that score line.

16. Make your way around the cover repeating Steps 11–15 on the remaining three corners as well as the spine [K].

17. Reposition your cover horizontally. Starting at the bottom right corner and working clockwise, place your triangle ruler at the intersection of the score lines then place the tip of your craft knife into the intersection. Line your triangle ruler up with your pencil mark at the bottom edge of the cover, then slice. Repeat until you have done this on all the corners and the spine [L+M].

I ↓

J ↓

K ↓

L ↓

M ↓

N ↓

O ↓

P ↓

Q ↓

Note → Now you are ready to create the buttonhole window on the spine. The window measurement is centred on the spine from top to bottom and is 2½ in/63 mm tall. I've chosen this specific measurement for the window because if it is taller, the sides of the window bulge out, and if it is shorter, the stitching becomes too loose.

18. Measure the height of your cover between the top and bottom score lines, halve that measurement and make a pencil mark at the centre of the spine.

19. Measure 1¼ in/32 mm up from the centre point and make a pencil mark. Do this again 1¼ in/32 mm down from the centre point [N].

20. With the spine facing you horizontally, position your triangle ruler flat on the spine with the base of the triangle ruler nestled into the spine score furthest from you and lift the front cover up so that your triangle ruler is square along the spine score. Draw a light pencil line from spine score to spine score. Repeat this step on the other side of the centre point pencil mark [O].

21. Position your triangle ruler on the pencil lines you just drew and score them with the tip of your bone folder [P].

22. Draw an X inside the window from corner to corner. Then use your ruler and craft knife to slice on the X. Go steady, as you don't want to slice beyond your spine score [Q].

Finish the cover and prepare for stitching ↓

Next you will tape in the buttonhole and spine flaps, reinforce your cover with the extra signature of Stonehenge, seal the flaps and prepare your signatures for stitching.

1. Place strips of double-adhesive tape on the flaps as shown. Separate one of your signatures and trim both pieces to 7¼ × 5¼ in/184 × 133 mm. Place a strip of double-adhesive tape to both folded pieces ⅛ in/3 mm from the folded edge [A+B].

2. Expose the adhesive strips around the buttonhole and the top and bottom spine flaps. Fold your buttonhole flaps down first, then the spine flaps [C].

3. Expose the adhesive strip on both of your trimmed signatures and place one trimmed signature adhesive side down ⅛ in/3 mm away from the buttonhole window and centred from top and bottom. Repeat on the opposite cover [D+E].

4. Expose the two strips of adhesive on your side flaps. Place the top and bottom flaps down first, then place your side flap over and press. Repeat on the other side. Press the cover under a heavy weight for about ten minutes. If you are using a glue stick, you will need to press the cover for longer [F+G].

5. Place your ten signatures inside the cover and jog the signatures to the surface against the spine and also the bottom. Doing this a couple of times is good and usually necessary, to be sure that your signatures are flush and aligned against the spine and bottom of your book [H].

6. Hold your book tightly so that the signatures don't move then take a pencil and draw a line at the top corner of the window from left to right. Repeat at the top of the window. Now you have your 'sewing stations' marked in pencil [I].

7. Set your cover aside and place your signatures to the side with the folds facing you [J].

8. Open the top signature and pierce through the marked sewing station at the top with your lightweight awl. Then rotate the signature and pierce through the bottom station [K].

9. Place your first signature with the fold facing away from you to one side and repeat the same steps for your remaining signatures [L].

A ↓   B ↓   C ↓   D ↓

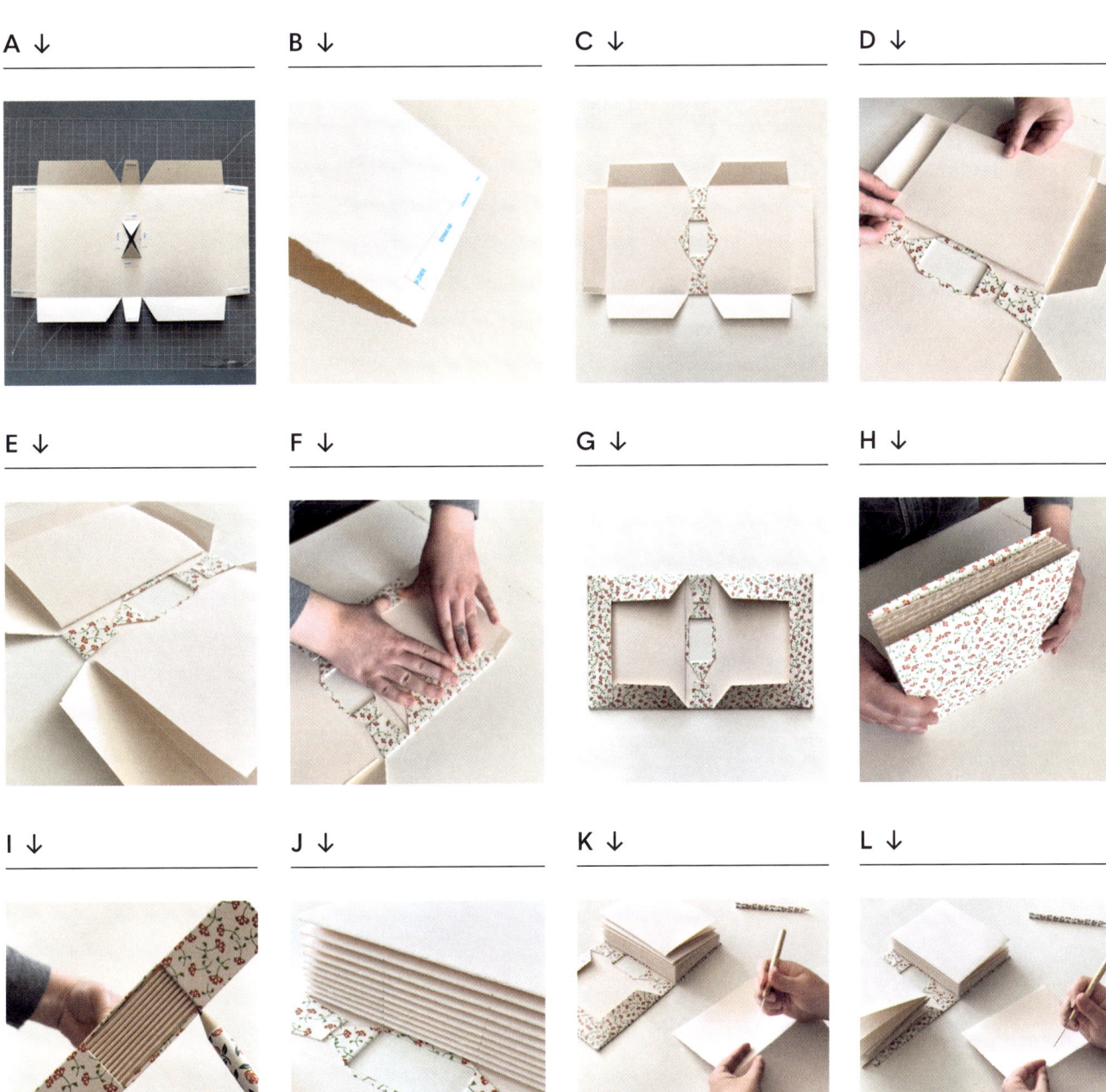

E ↓   F ↓   G ↓   H ↓

I ↓   J ↓   K ↓   L ↓

There are two things you need to know about stitching before you begin! First, you will be stitching from the back of the book forwards. Second, you stitch the top panel first with one length of thread, then you stitch the bottom panel with a separate length of thread.

Stitching tips →
1. Each time you come through the loop, you will pull down on the thread to tighten.
2. The stitch/knot naturally moves up as you pull down.
3. As you pull up on the thread, I suggest using your thumb to gently nestle the knot against the window's edge.

1. Determine your thread length: measure from the top of the book to the top of the window, times the number of signatures, times two, and add 6 in/15 cm for good measure. You can measure two lengths with this same measurement so the thread is on hand when you are ready to stitch your second panel [A].

2. Thread your needle. Take the bottom signature and position it up against the back cover [B].

3. Start on the inside of your signature and pull your thread through the hole you've made. Pull the thread through the window, leaving a tail of 3–4 in/7–10 cm on the inside of your signature [C].

4. Bring the long piece of thread around the top of the panel to the inside of the signature and tie off the thread at the sewing station with a double knot [D+E].

5. Exit through that same sewing station and pull the thread all the way through to the outside. Take your needle and go under the long stitch from right to left, pull it through until there's a little loop. Go through the loop from underneath, then pull down and tighten [F+G].

Stitching tip → When tightening the stitch, you may find it helpful to position the cover upright on your surface making it convenient to pull down on the thread. As you do this, the stitch will naturally slide up and tighten.

6. Take your second signature and place it up against the first. Enter the sewing station and pull the thread all the way through but leave a little loop on the outside [H].

7. Bring the thread up and around to the outside and to the right of the loop. Go through the loop from the bottom up (right to left). Then pull down and tighten.

Repeat Steps 6–7 until you reach the last signature [I–K].

8. When you complete your last signature you will be on the outside of the cover. Enter the station you just completed, pull the thread all the way through, take your needle and go under the inside stitch, leave a little loop and go through the loop, pull and tighten, then snip. You can leave as little as a ¼ in/0.5 cm of thread [L+M].

Repeat Steps 2–7 for the bottom of your book [N+O].

Note → Many students feel that stitching the bottom section is easier. You also get in the flow. Your bottom panel might look more evenly stitched than your top, and that is totally OK. Sometimes, I will pull out the first panel and re-stitch so that the panels look more consistent.

Happiness ensues!

A ↓

B ↓

C ↓

D ↓

E ↓

F ↓

G ↓

H ↓

I ↓

J ↓

K ↓

L ↓

M ↓

N ↓

O ↓

4

INTRODUCTION TO GLUEING HAPPINESS

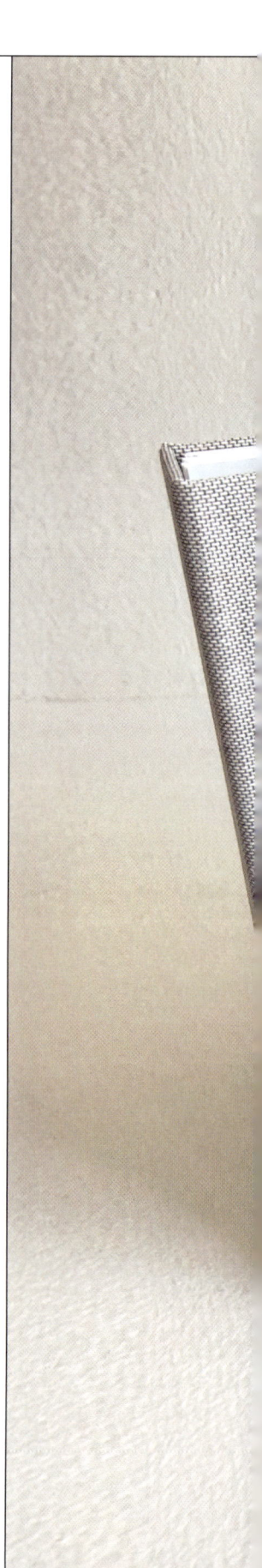

WHAT YOU'LL LEARN AND MAKE

Learn ↓

· Caring for your glue brush
· Glueing five distinctive
  bookbinding materials
· Making a hinged bookcover
· Wrapping a perfect corner
· Minimizing glueing mishaps

Make ↓

· Three hardcover padholder-folders
  measuring (4½ × 7½ × 1¼ in/114 ×
  190 × 31 mm)
· Three butterfly clips and
  three pencils wrapped with
  matching papers

Materials ↓

- 6 pieces of linen bookcloth for your outer and interior spine (3½ × 9 in/89 × 229 mm and 3½ × 7⅛ in/89 × 180 mm)
- 11 pieces of bookboard
  - 6 cover pieces (4¼ × 7¼ in/108 × 184 mm)
  - 3 spine pieces (1¼ × 7⅛ in/32 × 180 mm)
  - 2 small pieces to use for hinge corner spacer (1 × 5 in/25 × 127 mm)
- 4 sheets of Japanese Chiyogami decorative paper for your front, back and interior covers (two sized 4⅛ × 7⅛ in/105 × 180 mm, two sized 4⅛ × 9 in/105 × 229 mm)
- 4 sheets of Grafiche Tassotti decorative paper for your front, back and interior covers (two sized 4⅛ × 7⅛ in/105 × 180 mm, two sized 4⅛ × 9 in/105 × 229 mm)
- 4 sheets of hand-marbled decorative paper for your front, back and interior covers (two sized 4⅛ × 7⅛ in/105 × 180 mm, two sized 4⅛ × 9 in/105 × 229 mm)
- 3 stacklets of lovely drawing paper (small stacks for clipping into the inside of your folder)
- 3 sheets of each of the decorative papers for covering the clips and pencils (6¾ × 6 in/171 × 152 mm)
- 3 unsharpened pencils
- 3 medium butterfly clips
- 1 hinge and corner spacer (2 pieces of bookboard (1 × 5 in/254 × 127 mm) the same thickness as your cover, glued together))

Tools ↓

- bone folder
- Teflon bone folder (optional, but useful)
- craft knife
- metal ruler
- triangle ruler
- PVA glue
- glue brush
- a small cup for your glue
- scrap paper for glueing on
- a small cloth to keep your fingers clean
- a small wastepaper basket for your gluey scrap papers
- pencil
- cutting mat
- a cloth-covered brick (or heavy weight for pressing)

A FEW GLUEING HAPPINESS NOTES

Different papers ↓
This is the perfect opportunity to try out different styles of decorative papers. There are Japanese Chiyogami or Katazome papers (the most glue friendly), Cambridge Imprint papers, hand-marbled papers, or printed wrapping papers. They are all good for bookbinding. My recommendation is only on the weight of paper, which is best around 70 to 135 gsm.

Caring for your glue brush ↓
A fresh glue brush will come with a wire wrap around the bristles, which is removed prior to glueing. However, for as many decades as I've been glueing, I've always left it on, because the tighter the bristles, the more control you have over the glueing process.

I discovered that without the wire, the bristles splayed so significantly I ended up with a thick layer of glue on my cover paper that I couldn't thin out; this caused me to discard the materials I had been working with and start anew. That said, I'm a huge fan of experimentation. The tighter glue brush works for me, but it may not work for you, so I suggest you try it both ways.

If I'm working on a project where I'll be glueing several days in a row, I will cover the glue jar with plastic wrap and a very tight rubber band to keep the moisture in. When I'm finished, I run the brush and glue cup under warm water for a short time. Then I use a 3M Dobie sponge to scrub the excess glue off the wooden handle and metal base. When it is mostly clean, I will let the bristle portion of the brush rest in warm water for a few hours (sometimes overnight) to let the excess glue rinse out.

Glueing covers ↓
Whenever I'm in the midst of glueing and am about to flip my glued cover over after burnishing, I use a rag to be certain there's no glue on my surface or on my fingers. This is a very good glueing habit to have.

Glue boundaries ↓
These pencil lines keep the glue where you want it to be, and not where you don't, so I call them 'glue boundaries'. It's OK to glue over the pencil line, but try to stay close to them.

When PVA dries it can leave a light but noticeable film; if you haven't used glue boundaries and you've glued beyond where your cover will be placed, you'll need to glue over the film before glueing your book cover. This means that the paper or bookcloth may become thicker and more challenging to fold over the board smoothly. Depending on the paper, you might see a slightly raised area from the double layer of glue.

Conversely, you may not glue where you need to, which results in the paper or bookcloth puckering or lifting up. These mishaps can happen anytime, but the glue boundaries will help more often than not.

Seams ↓
If you brush your glue vertically along the edge of the fabric, glue will often get under and on your bookcloth. Even though your decorative paper will overlay where it meets the fabric, applying your glue off the edge of the sheet horizontally is a good habit to get into.

Glue the hardcover padholder-folder ↓

1. Pour an inch of PVA glue into a small cup.

2. Take a piece of scrap paper. Lift your glue brush from the cup. Scrape your brush on the side of the cup so it isn't laden with glue and begin brushing the glue on the scrap paper. Brush vertically then horizontally, smoothing out the glue ridges. You'll notice that the paper is buckling – some decorative papers will do this too. When you're working with new-to-you papers, it's always good to test them.

    Tip → Start with a light layer of glue. You can always add more.

3. Take one of your covers and make a pencil mark at the top and bottom 1 in/25 mm from the edge [A].

4. Position your bookcloth fabric side down, lining up the pencil marks on the edge of the fabric. Draw a pencil line onto the bookcloth around the cover, creating your glue boundaries [B].

5. Take your hinge spacer and place it snugly up against the first cover board, put your spine piece against the hinge spacer, remove the spacer and draw a pencil line around the spine piece. Place your hinge spacer on the left of the spine, place your second cover board up against the hinge spacer and draw a line around the cover [C+D].

6. Place a piece of scrap paper under your bookcloth and begin applying a light layer of glue to the spine and right panel, brushing your glue horizontally off the edge of the fabric. Remove the scrap paper after glueing [E].

7. Position your first cover piece on the glued fabric. Line up the two pencil marks with the edge of the bookcloth and press. Simultaneously position your hinge spacer snugly up against your first cover piece and your spine piece onto the bookcloth and up against the hinge spacer and press. Be sure your cover and spine are aligned at the top and bottom. I often place a ruler up against the top or bottom to be sure [F].

A ↓

B ↓

C ↓

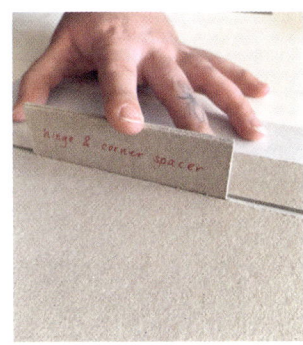

D ↓

E ↓

F ↓

8. Place a fresh piece of scrap paper under the unglued side of your bookcloth and apply a light layer of glue. Position your hinge spacer snugly up against the spine, take your second cover piece and position it up against the hinge spacer and press. Again, be sure your covers and spines are aligned at the top. Flip your cover over onto its underside and smooth out the fabric with the bone folder [G].

9. Place a piece of scrap paper under your cover, and swish a bit of glue on the top and bottom bookcloth flaps. Then remove the gluey paper from your surface and use either the surface or a Teflon bone folder to mould the bookcloth around the edge of your bottom cover [H].

10. Draw glue boundaries onto your two pieces of hand-marbled paper (4⅛ × 9 in/104 × 229 mm).

11. Place the paper decorative side down and position your cover so the edge of the paper overlaps your fabric by ¼ in/6 mm, then draw around the three sides of your cover. Do this for both pieces [I+J].

Note → When I'm glueing a paper without any orientation to the pattern I will often draw the glue boundaries using the cover on the same side. When your paper has a specific pattern that has a vertical orientation, for example, you will draw your glue boundaries by using both covers exactly as they will be glued. To help you maintain the orientation, make an 'X' at the top of each cover with a pencil.

12. Position your cover face down on your surface, close to where you are glueing. Take a piece of scrap paper and place it under your first piece of decorative paper, glue inside and a little over your glue boundaries.

13. Remove your glueing paper, then lift up your glued decorative paper and hover it over the cover to give yourself an aerial view. Line it up with the edge of the bookcloth, overlapping about ¼ in/6 mm. Once your paper is in place, press out any bubbles using a Teflon bone folder or the palm of your hand – be sure there isn't any glue on it! [K]

Tip → Some hand-marbled papers will bubble and go a bit wonky after you've applied glue. If the paper begins to buckle, lift it back up again and r-o-l-l it back down, smoothing it out as you go. I find this helps minimize bubbles and makes burnishing the paper easier.

G ↓

H ↓

I ↓

J ↓

Note → Most papers also like to lift up on the corners, so after glueing, give the corners a little extra pressing. Papers also like to lift up where the decorative paper meets the bookcloth. I will always smooth out with the Teflon bone folder, or even the palm of my hand or finger (first checking there's no glue on them).

14. Take your corner spacer and place it up against the top corner at a 45° angle. Draw a pencil line along the edge of the corner spacer, then use your craft knife to cut on the line. You can also cut directly along the corner spacer. Do the same for your opposite corner [L].

15. Take a piece of scrap paper, place it under your top and bottom flaps, swish a smidgen of glue on your flaps and then use the surface or Teflon bone folder to mould the paper around the cover [M].

16. Swish a light layer of glue on your fore-edge flap. Crimp in the corner nooks, which you can do with the tip of your bone folder or your fingertip. This creates a lovely finished look to your corners, resembling the bottom corner of an envelope [N].

Repeat Steps 11–16 for your back cover [O].

17. Take your inner spine bookcloth piece. Position it on the inside and confirm that there's frame of at least ⅛ in/1.6 mm at the top and bottom of the bookcloth.

K ↓

L ↓

M ↓

N ↓

O ↓

P ↓

Q ↓

R ↓

Tip → The next piece you will glue is your inner spine cloth. The top and bottom edges are visible, so here it's important that you glue off the edge at the top and bottom. Whenever I'm glueing a piece of bookcloth or paper where all four edges will be visible, I always begin glueing in the centre first, then brush off the edges in a star pattern. Glueing off the edge of all four sides of any material can cause the scrap paper underneath to move, and glue can get underneath it, onto your materials. I suggest lifting your brush as you go off the edge instead of continuing with the same pressure.

18. Place a piece of scrap paper under your inner spine bookcloth piece and begin glueing in the middle of the bookcloth, then off the edge at the sides, then the top and bottom. Lift up the bookcloth and hover it over the spine, to give yourself an aerial view. Make sure it's positioned evenly at the top and bottom, then press. Smooth out with your Teflon bone folder or the palm of your hand. Push gently into the hinge spaces [P].

19. Take one of your interior panels, place a piece of scrap paper underneath it and begin glueing. Start in the centre and use vertical then horizontal strokes, evenly and smoothly distributing the glue.

20. Lift the paper up, move your gluey paper aside, give yourself an aerial view and place the paper down lightly. Slowly and gently press the edges of the paper down to confirm you see a nice frame around all four edges. Once in place, burnish with your bone folder. Repeat on the other side [Q+R].

21. Press under a cloth-covered brick, or heavy weight.

Repeat Steps 1–21 to make a total of three hardcover padholder-folders.

Cover the clips and pencils ↓

1. Cover your butterfly clips exactly as you did in Chapter 2 (p.45) [A].

2. Place a piece of decorative paper up against your pencil. The paper should overlap the brass ferrule holding the eraser by about ⅛ in/1.6 mm and be flush with the unsharpened edge. Trim with your craft knife.

3. Roll the paper around the pencil with a little overlap and measure. Trim accordingly.

4. Place a piece of scrap paper under the decorative paper, glueing off the edge on all four sides. Remove the scrap paper, place the gluey paper glue side up [B].

Note → A light layer of glue is highly recommended here as the glue will squish out at the seam.

5. Position your pencil ⅛ in/1.6 mm from the edge, lining up the bottom end so it's flush. Begin rolling about ¼ in/6 mm, so that you can lift under the narrow flap and secure it to the pencil [C].

6. Keep rolling until you've reached the edge [D].

Wishing you many blissful Glueing Happiness moments!

A ↓

B ↓

C ↓

D ↓

5

CHIC CAMBRIDGE SUITE

WHAT YOU'LL MAKE

A pair of single-signature stitched hardcover folders with a soft fabric spine and angled interior pocket, and a Cambridge-coordinated set of butterfly clips. You can choose whether to affix your pocket inside the front or back cover.

Materials ↓

- 10 sheets of Cambridge Imprint 90 gsm patterned paper
    - 4 cover sheets (7¾ × 9¾ in/197 × 248 mm)
    - 2 interior panel sheets (5¾ × 7¾ in/146 × 197 mm)
    - 2 pocket back panel sheets (7¾ × 9¾ in/197 ×248 mm)
    - 2 front diagonal pocket sheets
      (6½ × 6½ in/165 × 165 mm)
- 4 pieces of bookboard (6 × 8 in/152 × 203 mm)
- 1 sheet of Stonehenge 250 gsm paper for your two 8-page signatures (22 × 30 in/559 × 762 mm)
- 3 sheets of Stonehenge for your pockets
    - 2 sheets measuring 5¾ × 7¾ in/146 × 197 mm
    - 1 sheet measuring 5 × 5 in/127 × 127 mm
- 4 pieces of bookcloth
    - outer spine piece (2 × 9½ in/51 × 241 mm)
    - inner spine piece (2 × 7½ in/51 × 191 mm)
- 2 lengths of 7-ply waxed linen thread (2 yd/1.8 m each)
- 7 (a binder's half-dozen) medium butterfly clips
- 1 sheet of Cambridge Imprint decorative paper to cover your clips (4 × 12 in/102 × 305 mm)
- 1 hinge and corner spacer (2 pieces of bookboard (1 × 5 in/254 × 127 mm) the same thickness as your cover, glued together)

Tools ↓

- bone folder
- Teflon bone folder
- shipping clerk's knife
- craft knife
- metal ruler
- triangle ruler
- lightweight awl
- medium awl
- size 18 embroidery needle
- PVA glue
- glue brush
- a cup for your glue
- scrap paper for glueing on
- a small cloth to keep your fingers glue free
- washi tape
- pencil
- scissors
- cutting mat
- a cloth-covered brick (or heavy book) for pressing your covers

Fold the signatures ↓

You will create two 8-page signatures (16 serendipitous sides).

Follow Steps 1–3 of **Folding signatures** (see **Techniques**, p.20). You now have four sheets, each measuring 11 × 15 in/279 × 381 mm.

Take one of your four pieces, fold it in half, slice again with your shipping clerk's knife, then take the two freshly cut sheets and use your working surface to line up the bottom edges. Use your bone folder to fold them in half, then set aside.

Repeat for your other three signatures, then merge two together to create your two 8-page signatures.

Glue the covers ↓

1. Begin by measuring and outlining your glue boundaries onto the back of your outer spine bookcloth pieces. Measure ⅝ in/16 mm from the edge of the bookboard at the top and bottom. Line those pencil marks up to the edge of the bookcloth and draw a pencil line around the cover [A].

2. Measure the thickness of your signature and add ⅜ in/9 mm. Once you have that measurement, place your other bookboard opposite the first and outline in pencil around that board [B].

> Note → If your bookcloth is wider on one cover than the other, now is a good time to trim. The measurement I used for my sample is ⅝ in/16 mm.

3. Take a piece of scrap paper, place it under the bookcloth. Apply an even swish of glue down the centre of your glue area on the right and then brush the glue horizontally off the edges, smoothing out your glue ridges [C].

4. Remove the scrap paper. Place your first cover piece onto the glued bookcloth and press.

5. Rotate your cover and glue the other side of the bookcloth, then gently position your second cover piece inside the pencil lines. Before you press, take your ruler and confirm the width of your spine is even at the top and bottom at 1¼ in/32 mm [D].

6. Flip your cover so that the fabric side is facing up and smooth out any bubbles that might have appeared under your bookcloth. Before you flip your cover back to fabric side down, be sure there's no glue on your surface.

7. Position your cover cloth-side down and place a piece of scrap paper under the top and bottom turn-ins.

8. Lightly swish some glue on both ends, then lift the cover and remove the gluey paper. Use your working surface to mould the turn-ins around the edge of the top of the cover, then repeat on the bottom, using your thumbs and forefingers and press the turn-ins down at the same time. Flip the cover around and repeat [E].

A ↓

B ↓

C ↓

D ↓

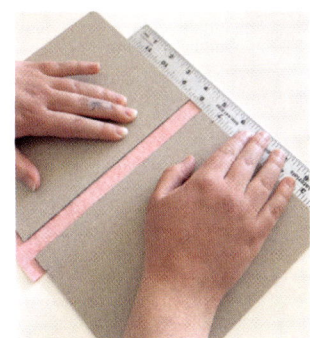

E ↓

Glue the decorative papers to the front and back covers ↓

> Note → Your decorative paper will overlap your bookcloth by ⅛ in/3 mm. It's totally OK if it overlaps a smidgen more – ⅛ in/3 mm is my minimum.

1. Take both of your cover papers and draw your glue boundaries.

> Note → Once you've brushed glue on your paper the corners will sometimes lift up. I suggest smoothing out the paper from the centre and then immediately pressing down on the corners. Then come back to burnish the cover again to smooth out any additional bubbles.

2. Place one of your decorative papers pattern side down, place a piece of scrap paper underneath and glue (going a little over the pencil lines is fine). Remove the gluey paper, then lift your paper with both hands and suspend it over the cover to give yourself an aerial view. Gently position the paper ⅛ in/3 mm over the fabric. Press and smooth out any bubbles [F].

3. Position your cover with the decorative side down. Deploy your corner spacer and place it up against the top corner at a 45° angle. Draw a pencil line. Do the same on the bottom corner [G].

4. Use your craft knife to trim along the pencil line. You can also use scissors if that feels more comfortable.

5. Next you will glue down your top and bottom flaps. Begin by placing a piece of scrap paper under your top and bottom flaps. Swish a light layer of glue and then move the glue paper aside and lift your cover up, using the surface to mould one side around your bookboard. Reverse the cover and repeat. While you're pressing one side onto the surface use your fingers and thumbs to press and secure the flap, then flip the cover around and secure the other flap in the same way.

    Note → For this side flap you don't need a lot of glue inside the nooks of your corners because the glue will only squish out, so go lightly. I prefer to use my fingernails for this part because I can feel the paper and the edges and corners of the boards, but you can use the tip of your bone folder for this step.

6. Place a piece of scrap paper under your side flap and then brush a light swish of glue. Remove the scrap paper. Crimp the nooks [H+I].

7. Use your working surface to mould the paper around the edge of the cover and then burnish with your bone folder [J].

Repeat Steps 1–7 to finish glueing the outer cover.

Finish the interior of the cover ↓

1. Position your interior spine bookcloth onto the spine (without glue) and reconfirm that you have an ⅛ in/3 mm border at the top and bottom of your cover and wide enough so that you have at least 1 in/25 mm stretching to the right and left interior covers [K].

2. Begin with a light swish of glue in the centre and brush out on all four edges, especially the top and bottom, as these edges will be seen.

F ↓

G ↓

H ↓

I ↓

J ↓

K ↓

Create inside pockets and glue in your interior panels ↓

1. Take your smaller sheet of Stonehenge (5 × 5 in/127 × 127 mm) and slice in half on the diagonal. This will create the exact size you need for the front piece of your pockets.

> Note → You will notice that the measurement is slightly smaller than your cover. That is deliberate so that once your pocket is glued in, there will be a nice border from the outer cover's decorative paper.

2. Next, outline your glue boundaries onto your two backing pieces and triangular pocket pieces [A].

3. Glue your Cambridge Imprint paper to the backing piece. Use your corner spacer to map where you will trim your corners [B+C].

4. Now glue the opposite side flaps down first. Use your forefinger or bone folder to crimp in the nooks of your corners [D+E].

5. Now glue your Cambridge Imprint paper to the triangular piece. See the illustration for how best to trim the three corners of the front piece [F+G].

6. Glue down the flap on the diagonal/long side of your pocket, and then glue the other two flaps and wrap them around to the back of the backing piece [H+I].

7. Glue in your interior decorative paper to the back cover (opposite side to the pocket, likely on the right-hand side) [J].

A ↓

B ↓

C ↓

D ↓

E ↓

F ↓

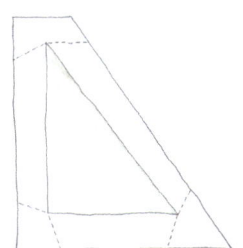

G ↓

H ↓

> Note → All four edges will be seen so the best way to glue these two pieces is to start in the centre and glue out in a star pattern, so that you are glueing off the edge on all four sides.

8. Glue your pocket panel to the inside of the front cover. Simply place the panel onto a piece of scrap paper. Begin in the middle of the panel and glue out to the edges, but not too close. Leave at least ¼ in/6 mm border otherwise when you add the weight for pressing, the glue could squish out. If it does that, just use a cotton bud (Q-tip) and carefully lift the glue residue [K].

9. Give yourself an aerial view and place the pocket panel on the inside cover so that it's evenly placed, then press with your heavy weight and let dry for a minimum of two hours.

Repeat Steps 1–9 for your second cover.

Create the stitching template ↓

1. Trim a piece of Stonehenge to the height and width of your spine.

2. Draw a pencil line directly down the centre of the template from top to bottom.

3. Position your template and ruler horizontally in front of you. Begin by making a pencil dot ½ in/13 mm from the top. Make a pencil mark every ½ in/13 mm as you make your way down the template. Your last dot will be at 7½ in/191 mm and you will have 15 sewing stations [A].

4. Pierce holes into the template using your medium awl [B].

5. Use your lightweight awl to widen them a bit more [C].

6. Attach the template to the interior of the spine with a bit of washi tape. Take your medium awl and pierce through the template sewing stations onto the spine itself. Then use your lightweight awl to widen them a bit more for ease of stitching [D].

7. Transfer the sewing stations onto the spine of your signature. Mark them with a pencil first, then use your lightweight awl to pierce your signature [E+F].

A ↓

B ↓

C ↓

D ↓

E ↓

F ↓

Stitch using the Cambridge hitch stitch ↓

1. Measure a piece of thread five times the height of your book, then thread your needle.

2. Start on the inside of your signature and exit station 1 at the top of the spine. Pull the thread until you have a 4 in/10 cm tail [A].

3. Enter station 2. Exit station 1 again [B+C].

> Note → At this point, we are tying off at station 2. I have discovered that because the anchoring stitch is wound around stations 1 and 2, it's not necessary to tie off. Ruby, my nimble studio/shop assistant, thinks it looks tidier without a knot, and I've come to agree. Experiment and see which you prefer!

4. Enter station 2 again and tie a half knot there. Exit station 3. This is your anchor stitch [D–F].

5. Go behind the stitch from right to left [G].

6. Enter station 4 and exit station 3 [H+I].

7. Go behind the stitch from left to right. Enter station 5. Exit station 4 [J].

8. Continue stitching by alternating the 'go behind' from right to left, and then left to right. When you get to the bottom you will enter station 15 and tie off on the inside by threading your needle behind the last interior stitch [K–O].

Stitch your second book in the same way. Cover your butterfly clips as you did in Chapter 2 (p.45).

A ↓

B ↓

C ↓

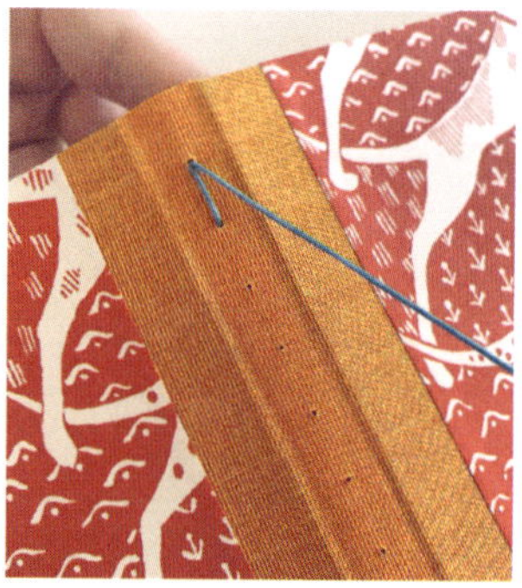

D ↓

E ↓

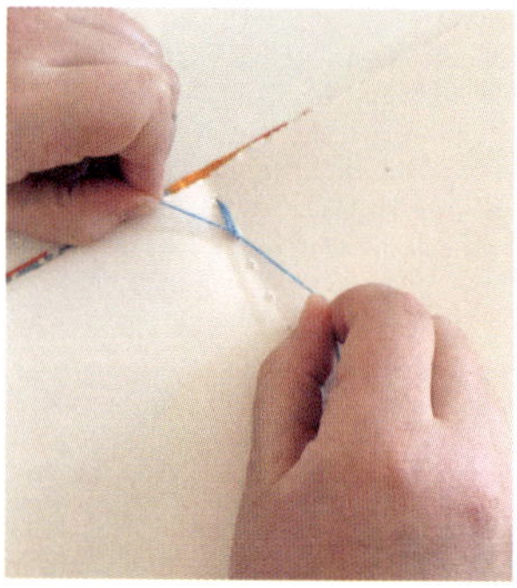

F ↓

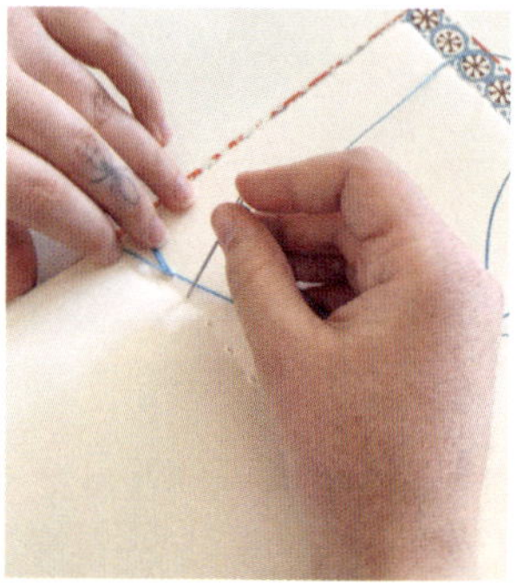

G ↓

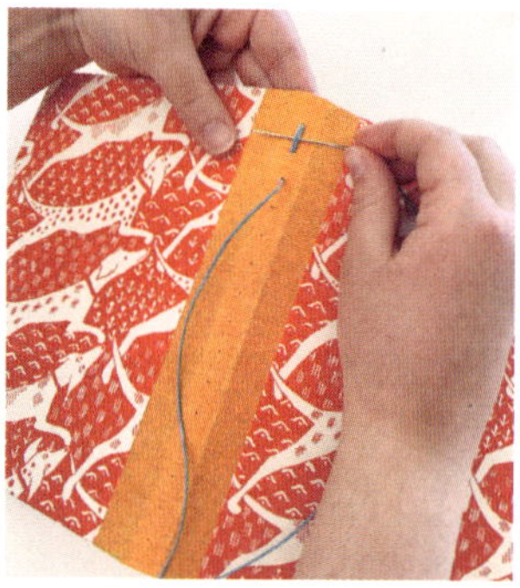

H ↓

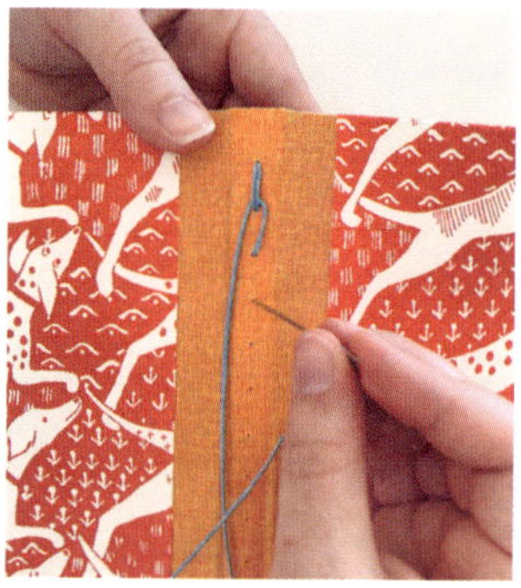

I ↓

J ↓

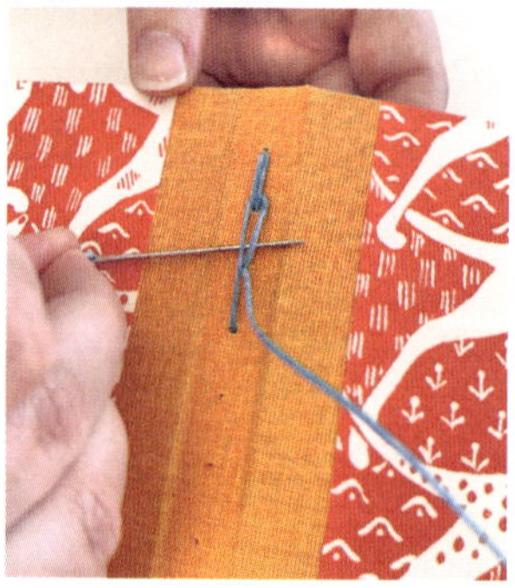

K ↓

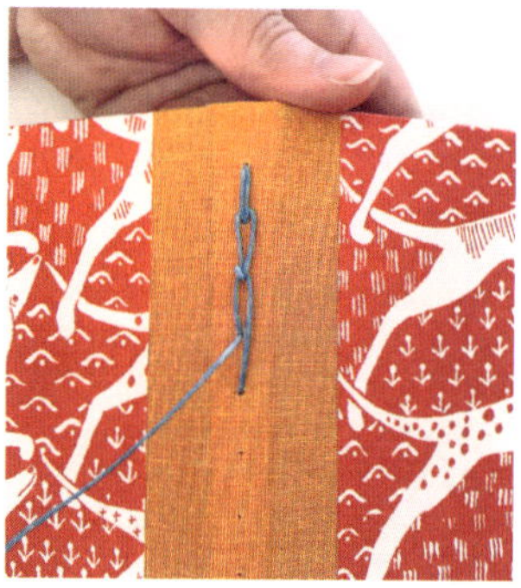

L ↓

M ↓

N ↓

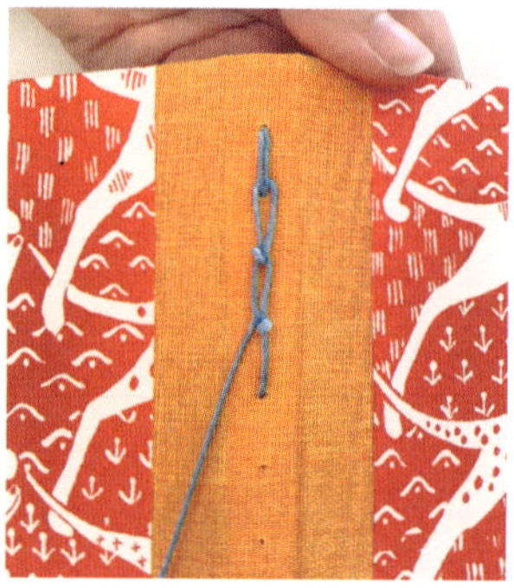

O ↓

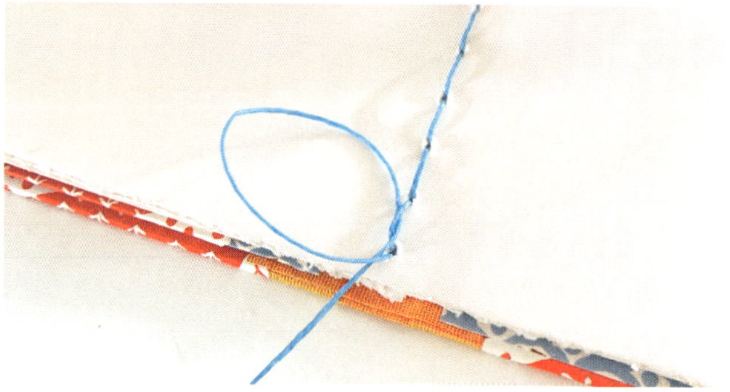

In this chapter you will learn three different styles of hinging your accordion panels. In the first book, I demonstrate a very basic technique, because the spine of the book is completely enclosed within an external paper spine. The second book is made with hardcovers and without an external spine, using a traditional hinging technique. The third book has an articulated cover, interior pocket and a string-and-button closure.

A TRIO OF CONCERTINA TECHNIQUES

A TRIO OF ORIGAMI-ESQUE ACCORDION BOOKS

Three 5 × 5 × 1 in/127 × 127 × 25 mm accordion books with 18 pages (nine 2-sided panels). Each book fans open to about a yard/metre long, and will stand gracefully without support. They make lovely journals, excellent photo albums and brilliant swatch keepers. An accordion is also great for collage, calligraphy, photos and ephemera, and any combination thereof.

Skill Level → ●●●○○

Materials ↓

- 15 sheets of Stonehenge 250 gsm paper (5 × 20 in/127 × 508 mm)
- 15 sheets of Fabriano Tiziano 160 gsm paper
    - 12 cover papers (5 × 10 in/127 × 254 mm)
    - 3 spine papers (5 × 5 in/127 × 127 mm)
- 6 pieces of Bristol board or chipboard (5 × 5 in/127 × 127 mm)

Tools ↓

- bone folder
- craft knife
- metal ruler
- triangle ruler
- pencil
- scissors
- double-adhesive tape (½ in/13 mm wide)

Fold the accordions ↓

1. Position one sheet of Stonehenge horizontally. Fold it over onto itself, lining up the four corners on the left, and crease with your bone folder [A].

2. Rotate your paper 180° and fold the top piece over, lining up the four corners, and crease with your bone folder [B].

3. Now flip your paper over and repeat on the other side. You now have one 4-panel accordion measuring 5 × 5 in/127 × 127 mm [C].

Repeat Steps 1–3 with your remaining sheets of Stonehenge.

A ↓

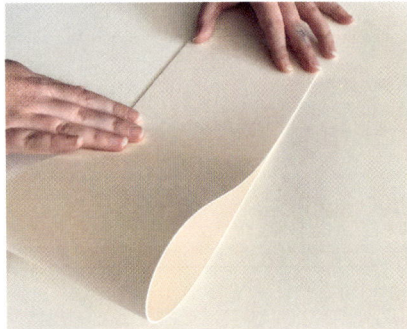

B ↓

C ↓

Fold the cover papers ↓

1. Take one piece of Fabriano Tiziano cover paper (5 × 10 in/127 × 254 mm) and position it on your surface horizontally. Place a piece of chipboard in the centre of the cover paper [A].

2. Use your bone folder and make a score line against the chipboard. Remove the chipboard, fold the cover paper over at the score line and crease with your bone folder [B].

3. Nestle the chipboard inside the fold. Use your bone folder and score against the opposite edge. Remove the chipboard and fold at the score line [C].

Repeat Steps 1– 3 with your remaining cover papers.

A ↓

B ↓

C ↓

Assemble the covers ↓

1. Use your scissors or craft knife to trim the flaps on six of your covers. Taper the flaps ¼ in/6 mm (roughly) to the centre fold line [A].

2. Take one of the untrimmed cover papers and fold it around a piece of chipboard [B].

3. Take one of the trimmed cover papers and slide one flap between the chipboard and the untrimmed cover paper [C].

Repeat with the other flap [D].

Note → Slightly curve the cover so you can slide the second flap into the opposite opening of the cover. After you've interlocked the two cover papers around the board, you might notice that it puffs out a little – this is perfectly normal.

A ↓

B ↓

C ↓

D ↓

Hinge the accordions ↓

1. Line up the panels of one of your accordions so they fan out in three rows with the top and bottom straight edges facing you.

2. Place a strip of double-adhesive tape on the edges of four panels, leaving the top one without adhesive [A].

3. Gather the top two panels – one with adhesive and one without – expose the adhesive, gently align the panels, then press them together [B].

4. Attach the next accordion by placing it up against the back of the first two and press. [C].

Repeat Steps 1–4 with the two remaining accordions.

A ↓

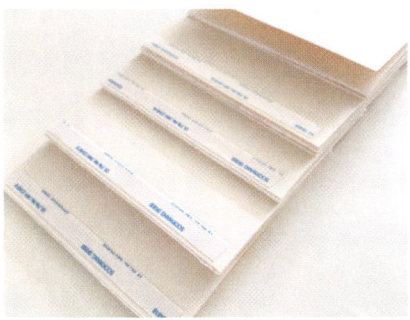

B ↓

C ↓

Interlock the accordions to the cover and attach the spine ↓

1. Taper the first and last panels of your accordion down towards the fold line [A].

2. Slide one end panel inside the cover between the straight edge and the folded edge. Repeat with the other end panel [B].

3. Place your accordion book flat on the working surface. Measure the thickness of your accordion where the bottom panel meets the cover [C].

4. Take one spine paper (5 × 5 in/127 × 127 mm) and place your triangle ruler ⅓ in/8 mm from the right edge and score with the tip of your bone folder. Fold over and press, and open flat [D].

5. Place the triangle ruler to the left of the first spine score and measure the distance of your spine thickness, plus a smidgen. Score with the tip of your bone folder, fold and crease. (For reference, my spine width is 1 in/25 mm) [E].

6. Trim both flaps of the spine piece. Add a strip of adhesive to each flap [F].

7. Expose the adhesive and slide one flap between the spine of the accordion and the cover. Repeat on the other side [G].

Repeat Steps 1–7 to complete your other two accordion books.

A ↓

B ↓

C ↓

D ↓

E ↓

F ↓

G ↓

TRADITIONAL ACCORDION BOOK

A traditional accordion book that measures 6⅛ × 6⅛ × ¾ in/156 × 156 × 19 mm when closed. When completely open it will span about 6 ft/1.8 m! When slightly folded, it will stand unsupported, and measure between 3–4 ft/0.9–1.25 m. You will learn to recess a 2 × 2 in/51 × 51 mm window in your front cover, to which you can affix a card with a title or a mini-collage.

Materials ↓

- 5 sheets of Stonehenge 250 gsm paper (6 × 20 in/152 × 508 mm)
- 2 pieces of bookboard (6⅛ × 6⅛ in/156 × 156 mm)
- 2 pieces of decorative paper (8 × 8 in/203 × 203 mm). I used Katazome 70 gsm paper.
- waxed paper
- 4 hinges (70 lb/105 gsm text paper trimmed to ¾ × 6 in/19 × 152 mm)
- 1 corner spacer (2 pieces of bookboard (1 × 5 in/254 × 127 mm) the same thickness as your cover, glued together)

Tools ↓

- bone folder
- Teflon bone folder
- craft knife
- metal ruler
- triangle ruler
- PVA glue
- glue brush
- glue stick
- scrap paper for glueing on
- a cup for your glue
- a small cloth to keep your fingers glue free
- pencil
- cutting mat

Measure, score and fold the accordion panels ↓

1. Begin by trimming the deckled edge off one side of your panels. Position one sheet of Stonehenge horizontally, with the trimmed edge on the right. Measure 6 in/152 mm from the right edge of your panel, use the tip of your bone folder to score, fold over and open back up again [A].

> Note → You don't need to fold and open flat as you go, but it makes it easier to see the score line, which will help you measure the following score lines.

2. Line up your triangle ruler at the bottom edge of the accordion panel and use your metal ruler to measure 6 in/152 mm just to the left of the score line.

3. Continue scoring at the 6 in/152 mm plus a smidgen three times. You will end up with a bit of extra tab which you will trim next [B].

Repeat Steps 1–3 on the remaining sheets of Stonehenge.

4. Place your folded accordion flat on the surface, and line your triangle ruler up against the folds, to secure the panel you are trimming.

5. Lift the top accordion panels away, giving you the room you need to trim with your craft knife [C].

Hinge the accordions on the inside edges of the panels (traditional) ↓

1. Take your four hinges and use your bone folder and triangle ruler to score them down the centre at ⅜ in/9 mm. Fold them in half and set them aside [D].

2. Take two accordion panels and place them upright on the working surface. Rest one of the hinges on the edge of a piece of slim scrap paper. Place another piece of scrap paper under the hinge [E].

3. Deploy your glue stick and swish a layer of glue on the left-hand outside flap.

4. Place the hinge on the edge of your first panel. Be sure that the fold of the hinge is lined up with the edge of the accordion [F].

5. Take two more pieces of scrap paper, placing one under the hinge and one under the accordion panel with the attached hinge [G].

6. Deploy your glue stick and swish a layer of glue on the attached hinge. Take your second accordion and line up the two edges [H].

Repeat Steps 1–6 with the remaining panels.

A ↓

B ↓

C ↓

D ↓

E ↓

F ↓

G ↓

H ↓

Hinge the accordions on the outside edges of the panels (optional) ↓

A ↓

B ↓

1. Place the scored and folded hinge on a piece of scrap paper. Swish a light layer of glue with your glue stick.

2. Take two panels with the edges facing each other and enclose the hinge around the edge [A].

3. Mould the hinge around and press [B].

Repeat Steps 1–3 with the remaining accordions.

Create a square recess in the cover ↓

1. Cut a piece of scrap paper 2 × 2 in/5 × 5 cm.

2. Position the scrap on the cover where you'd like the recess to be [A].

> Note → If you'd like the recess centred vertically, you'll want a bit more space at the bottom. If you place it centrally on the paper, you will notice that it looks lower on the cover than it is in reality.

> Note → You'll want your recess area to be a smidgen larger than the scrap piece so that your label drops into the recess.

3. Draw a pencil line around the scrap piece [B].

4. Take your triangle ruler and redraw the pencil lines so that they are squared off [C].

5. Position your triangle ruler at the bottom of the cover, ensuring that your first cut into the board will be squared with the cover. As you rotate your cover, line up your triangle ruler along the edge each time.

6. Use the tip of your craft knife to lift a corner of the board and peel away. Depending on the make of board, the recess may come off in one go, but I will often need to use the tip of my craft knife to lift up each corner [D+E].

7. Once you've lifted away enough so that you see a depressed edge, use the square tip of your Teflon bone folder to smooth/burnish the exposed board [F].

A ↓

B ↓

C ↓

D ↓

E ↓

F ↓

> Note → Depending on the thickness and make of your bookboard, you will only need to run your craft knife a few times over the cover to make a little slice into it.

Glue the covers ↓

1. Place one of your cover papers on the surface, decorative side down.

2. Use your pencil to draw glue boundaries around the edge of the bookboard. Do this for both covers [A].

3. Begin by glueing your back cover. Brush a light layer of glue onto the paper, just a smidgen over the pencil lines [B].

4. Place the bookboard without the recess onto the paper and press. Flip the cover over and use your Teflon bone folder to burnish the decorative paper [C].

5. Place a corner spacer at a 45° angle at each of the top and bottom corners and draw a pencil line, then trim with your craft knife [D].

6. Place a piece of scrap paper under the cover and swish a light layer of glue on two opposite flaps, then mould them around to the inside of the cover [E].

7. Place a piece of scrap paper under one side flap, and swish a light layer of glue. Crimp in the corners with your bone folder (or forefinger), then mould it around to the inside of the cover. Repeat on the opposite flap [F].

Note → For glueing the cover with a recess you will place the paper down as usual. After placing the glued paper onto the bookboard, I like to use the palm of my hand to press into the recessed area. Then I use the square tip of my Teflon bone folder to press into the edges for a crisp finish.

Repeat Steps 1–7 for the second cover.

8. Use your Teflon bone folder to mould the decorative paper into the recessed edge [G].

A ↓

B ↓

C ↓

D ↓

E ↓

F ↓

G ↓

Glue in the accordion ↓

1. Place your covers to one side of your glueing area. Position your accordion book flat on the surface and place a piece of scrap paper under one end panel. Brush PVA glue in the centre and then outwards in a star pattern [A].

2. Place your back cover with the interior panel facing up and position the glued accordion page onto the cover, being sure it's evenly placed. Press and burnish the panel with your Teflon bone folder [B].

3. Place a piece of waxed paper inside the back cover while you repeat Step 3 for the front cover. The waxed paper helps keep the moisture from the glue away from your second panel [C].

4. After you've glued in your second panel, place a heavy weight on each of the covers with your accordion upright, until dry [D].

A ↓

B ↓

C ↓

D ↓

DROP-SPINE ACCORDION BOOK

A drop-spine landscape accordion book measuring 4¾ × 5½ × 1¼ in/121 × 140 × 32 mm. The hinged book cover encloses and protects the accordion pages. The front cover and spine do not attach directly to the accordion panel-block; instead, the back cover features a vertical pocket to hold your book in place while using and displaying it. The pocket also enables you to insert fresh accordion panel-blocks as you fill them up.

Skill Level → ● ● ● ● ○

Materials ↓

- 6 sheets of Stonehenge 250 gsm paper (4½ × 22 in/114 × 559 mm)
- 5 pieces of bookboard
    - 2 cover pieces (4¾ × 5½ in/121 × 140 mm)
    - 1 spine piece (1¼ × 4¾ in/32 × 121 mm)
    - 2 hinge spacer pieces (1 × 5 in/254 × 127 mm)
- 2 pieces of bookcloth
    - outside spine (4 × 6¼ in/102 × 159 mm)
    - inside spine (4 × 4⅜ in/102 × 111 mm)
- 5 sheets of Japanese 70 gsm decorative paper
    - 2 cover sheets (5½ × 6½ in/140 × 165 mm)
    - 1 front interior sheet (4½ × 5¼ in/114 × 133 mm)
    - 2 back pocket sheets
        - back panel (6 × 7 in/152 × 178 mm)
        - front of pocket (6 × 6 in/152 × 152 mm)
- 2 sheets of Stonehenge for the pocket
    - 1 back panel piece (4½ × 5¼ in/114 × 133 mm)
    - 1 front pocket piece (4 × 4½ in/102 × 114 mm)
- 5 paper hinges (¾ × 4½ in/19 × 114 mm)
- 1 length waxed linen thread (18 in/46 cm)
- 1 sweet button (¾ in/19 mm)
- 1 hinge and corner spacer (2 pieces of bookboard (1 × 5 in/254 × 127 mm) the same thickness as your cover, glued together)

Tools ↓

- bone folder
- Teflon bone folder
- craft knife
- metal ruler
- triangle ruler
- medium awl
- PVA glue
- glue brush
- a cup for your glue
- scrap paper for glueing on
- a small cloth to keep your fingers glue free
- glue stick
- pencil
- scissors
- cutting mat
- a cloth-covered brick or heavy weight for pressing your covers

Measure, score and fold the accordion panels ↓

1. Fold your panels as you did for the **Traditional Accordion** book (on p.90). The measurement for each of these panels is 5¼ in/133 mm wide. You will fold each three times and each accordion will have four panels. You will have a smidgen extra at the end, which you will trim away.

2. Hinge your accordion panels as you did for the **Traditional Accordion** book. If you choose visible hinges, you could absolutely use decorative paper for a colourful edge.

Glue the cover ↓

1. Make a pencil mark at the top and bottom of one of your covers at 1 in/25 mm from the edge. Place a piece of bookcloth fabric side down, lining up the pencil marks on the edge of the fabric. Use a pencil to draw a line around the cover, onto the bookcloth, to create glue boundaries [A].

2. Take a hinge spacer and place it snugly up against the first cover board. Put your spine piece against the hinge spacer, then remove the spacer and draw a pencil line around the spine piece.

3. Place the hinge spacer on the left of the spine, place your second cover board up against it, and draw a line around the cover [B].

4. Place a piece of scrap paper under your bookcloth and begin glueing the spine and the area to the right of the spine. Brush your glue horizontally off the edge of the fabric, remove

the scrap paper, line up the two pencil marks with the edge of the bookcloth and press [C].

Note → Be sure your cover and spine are aligned at the top and bottom. I often place a ruler up against the top or bottom to level them.
----

5. Position the hinge spacer snug up against your cover, position your spine piece onto the bookcloth and up against the hinge spacer simultaneously, and press [D].

6. Place a fresh piece of scrap paper under the unglued side of your bookcloth and brush on a light layer of glue. Position the hinge spacer snugly up against the spine, take your second cover piece and position it up against the hinge spacer, and press. Again, be sure your covers and spines are aligned at the top. Flip

A ↓

B ↓

C ↓

D ↓

your cover over and smooth out the fabric with the bone folder [E].

7. Making sure there's no glue residue on the working surface, place your cover bookcloth side down with a piece of scrap paper underneath it, and swish a bit of glue on your top and bottom spine flaps. Remove the gluey scrap paper from your surface, then use the surface or your Teflon bone folder to mould the bookcloth around the edge of your bottom cover [F].

8. Take two pieces of Japanese decorative paper and draw your glue boundaries. Place the paper decorative side down and position your cover so the edge of the paper overlaps your fabric by ⅛ in/3 mm, and draw around your cover with your pencil [G].

9. Position your cover fabric side up. Take a piece of scrap paper and place it under your first piece of decorative paper. Glue inside your glue boundaries (and a little over).

10. Remove your gluey paper, then lift up your decorative paper to give yourself an aerial view, and line it up with the edge of the bookcloth, overlapping by about ⅛ in/3 mm. Once your paper is in place, press out any bubbles using your Teflon bone folder or the palm of your hand.

11. Take the corner spacer and place it up against the top corner at a 45° angle, draw a pencil line along the edge of the corner spacer, then use your craft knife to cut on the line. Repeat on the bottom corner [H].

12. Place a piece of scrap paper under your top and bottom flaps, swish a light layer of glue on your flaps and then use the surface or your Teflon bone folder to mould the paper around the cover [I].

E ↓

F ↓

G ↓

H ↓

13. Swish a light layer of glue on your fore-edge flap. Use the tip of your bone folder or your fingertips to crimp in the corner nooks. This step gives a lovely finished look to your corners.

Repeat Steps 8–13 for your back cover.

14. Place your interior spine piece on a piece of scrap paper. Begin glueing in the centre and brush off the edge on all four sides. Move your gluey paper aside and lift up the spine piece to give yourself an aerial view. Position the spine piece so that the top and bottom edges are evenly placed, then press and burnish with your bone folder [J].

15. Smooth out the hinged area with your thumb, forefingers or bone folder [K].

Attach the button ↓

1. Place your button on the cover about 1 in/2.5 cm from the right edge. Use your ruler to be sure the placement is also even vertically.

2. Take your pencil and make dots through the buttonholes onto the cover. You could bypass the pencil step and use the medium awl to make a little indentation – try both to see which works better for you [A]!

3. Use your medium awl to pierce the buttonholes through the front cover [B].

4. Next, line up the back cover with the placement of the front cover button. Use your medium awl to pierce two identical holes through the back cover.

5. Trim a piece of waxed linen thread to 6 in/15 cm and thread the button onto the front cover. Tie a double knot on the inside [C].

6. Trim the tails to ¼ in/0.5 cm, then press with the Teflon bone folder to flatten the bulge of the knot.

7. For the back, you will use a 12 in/30 cm length of waxed linen thread. Begin on the outside of the cover and enter one hole, then come out of the other. Tie a half knot, then, with the longer piece of thread, go back out of the hole closest to the fore-edge [D].

A ↓

B ↓

C ↓

D ↓

Make the back pocket and glue in the interior panels ↓

1. Take your 4½ × 5¼ in/114 × 133 mm piece of Stonehenge and 6 × 7 in/152 × 178 mm sheet of Japanese decorative paper. Place the decorative paper on the surface decorative side down, with the Stonehenge on top. Draw your glue boundaries.

   Note → The exposed area of Stonehenge will not be seen. If you glued the Japanese paper around completely, then the end side of the pocket would become too bulky.

2. Glue your decorative paper within the pencil lines and then place your Stonehenge piece onto the paper and press. Flip it over and smooth out any bubbles.

3. Place your back panel with the back facing up and use your corner spacer to measure and then trim your corners [A].

4. Glue the three flaps to the back of the panel [B].

5. Take your 4 × 4½ in/102 × 114 mm piece of Stonehenge and 6 × 6 in/152 × 152 mm piece of Japanese decorative paper and draw your glue boundaries as you did in Step 1 [C].

6. Glue your decorative paper within the pencil lines and then place your Stonehenge piece onto the paper and press. Flip it over and smooth out any bubbles.

7. Trim the pocket corners. The corners of this panel are trimmed differently from your traditional corners. See photo for reference [D].

8. I've numbered each side to show the order in which to glue them [E].

9. Glue one short edge flap to the back of the pocket, leaving you with three unglued flaps [F].

10. Glue the opposite short flap onto the back panel (decorative face down) and line it up against the edge of the pocket panel. Mould the opposite short glued flap around to the back of the back panel [G+H].

A ↓

B ↓

C ↓

D ↓

E ↓

F ↓

G ↓

H ↓

I ↓

J ↓

K ↓

L ↓

11. Glue your top and bottom flaps and mould those to the back of the back panel. Set the pocket aside [I].

12. Glue your 4½ × 5¼ in/114 × 133 mm sheet of decorative paper to the inside front cover [J].

13. Place the pocket panel onto a piece of scrap paper. Begin glueing in the middle of the panel and then spread out towards the edges.

Note → Leave at least ¼ in/0.5 cm border when glueing, otherwise the glue could squish out when you press it. If it does that, just use a cotton bud (Q-tip) to carefully lift the glue residue.

14. Give yourself an aerial view and place the pocket panel on the inside back cover. Press the whole cover with a heavy weight and let it dry for a minimum of two hours [K].

M ↓

Finishing touches ↓

1. Once dry and pressed, slide the back panel of your accordion into the pocket. If there's any resistance, trim the back panel to allow the accordion to slide in more smoothly [L].

2. Wind the waxed linen thread around the button a couple of times and tie a half knot directly below where you snip the extra thread [M].

Enjoy!

7

SCREW-POST ALBUM WITH WINDOW

WHAT YOU'LL MAKE

A screw-post binder measuring 8 × 8 × 1 in/203 × 203 × 25 mm with a 2 × 2 in/51 × 51 mm window in the front cover. This is a great binding style for single-sheet (unfolded) pages, whether they are pre-printed or blank. Pages are held in place by the screw-post spine piece. It is easy to resequence, remove or replace pages as you wish.

Skill Level → ● ● ● ○ ○

Materials ↓

- 3 pieces of pre-cut bookboard
    - 2 pieces (8⅛ × 8¼ in/206 × 210 mm)
    - 1 piece (8¼ × 1 in/210 × 25 mm)
- 1 stack of 80 lb/120 gsm text paper (8 × 8 in/203 × 203 mm) for your pages (½ in/13 mm)
- 2 pieces of Japanese bookcloth
    - 1 interior spine piece (8 × 10 in/203 × 254 mm)
    - 1 outer spine piece (4 × 10 in/102 × 254 mm)
- 4 sheets of Japanese 70 gsm decorative paper
    - 2 cover pieces (8 × 10 in/203 × 254 mm)
    - 2 interior panel pieces (8 × 8 in/203 × 203 mm)
- 3 strips of Crescent board for your interior spine piece (¾ × 8 in/19 × 203 mm)
- 3 aluminium screw posts (¾ in/20 mm)
- 1 hinge and corner spacer (2 pieces of bookboard (1 × 5 in/254 × 127 mm) the same thickness as your cover, glued together)

Tools ↓

- bone folder
- Teflon bone folder
- craft knife
- metal ruler
- triangle ruler
- PVA glue
- glue brush
- a cup for your glue
- scrap paper for glueing on
- a small cloth to keep your fingers glue free
- pencil
- cutting mat
- washi or painter's tape
- a standard three-hole punch with adjustable hole placements
- a mini (or maxi) Tandy Leather hole punch
- scissors
- a cloth-covered brick or heavy weight for pressing your covers
- marker pen
- double-adhesive tape

Arrange the covers and pages ↓

Because the pages are square, and the covers are only slightly larger and not exactly square, be sure covers and spine are correctly oriented before glueing [A].

Once you have everything in place, pencil an 'X' at the top of the covers and draw a line down the spine side of one sheet of paper. I like to draw a pencil line down the left margin of the sheet as well; this way it's easy to match up the pages and the cover once you have finished glueing. I will also sketch an outline of the paper position on the board itself [B].

Note → We will be making the book around the pages that we're binding so prioritise following the instructions rather than the actual measurements in this project.

Note → I use one of the pages as a guide when drawing the line, but you could also use the spine board.

Create the inner spine piece ↓

1. Place your 8 × 10 in/203 × 254 mm bookcloth fabric side down. Place your scrap paper to the left or right of your bookcloth, depending where it will be most comfortable for glueing.

2. Measure your stack of pages (½ in/13 mm if following these instructions), add ⅜ in/9 mm and make a note of this measurement.

3. Measure 2 in/51 mm from the right edge, place a piece of Crescent board on the bookcloth and draw your glue boundary. Place another Crescent board piece your noted measurement to the left of the first on the bookcloth and draw your glue boundary. Finally, place the third piece of Crescent board

⅛ in/3 mm to the left and draw your last glue boundary [C].

Note → These pencil lines are just to guide you when glueing. I recommend following the measuring steps again as you glue and place down your Crescent board pieces.

4. Place the three pieces of Crescent board 1 in/2.5 cm apart on the scrap paper and apply glue to each one.

A ↓

B ↓

C ↓

D ↓

5. Position the first piece of Crescent board 2 in/51 mm from the right edge of the bookcloth, centred vertically [D].

6. Position your two rulers, one at the top and one at the bottom of the first piece of Crescent board.

7. Take your second piece of Crescent board and place it down lightly on the bookcloth to the left of the first using the measurement noted in Step 3. Before you press, confirm the distance is equal at the top and bottom, then press [E].

8. Take the third piece of Crescent board and place it ⅛ in/3 mm to the left of the second piece. This gives you enough hinge area that these two pieces fold over without bulging out.

9. Flip the piece over and smooth out the cloth, then turn it fabric side down, but first be sure that there's no glue on your surface!

10. Trim your corners [F]. On the following page is a charming illustration to follow too.

E ↓

F ↓

G ↓

H ↓

I ↓

J ↓

K ↓

L ↓

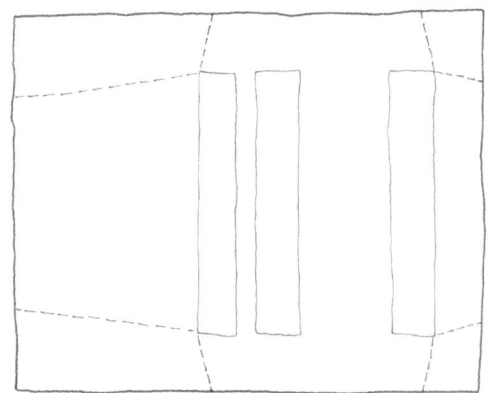

Note → I like to mould the fabric around the boards before I glue down the side flaps, as these creases create your glue boundaries [G].

11. Glue down the top and bottom flaps, then glue your side flaps to the board [H+I].

12. Fold the spine piece so that your single side is folded down and the double hinged side is folded into the centre [J–L].

13. You may find that there's more bookcloth flap on one side than the other, so you'll want to trim the flaps to even them out. A good width is 1½ in/3.8 mm.

Create the window ↓

1. Take one of the covers with an 'X' at the top. Measure the distance of the 'spine' of where the bookcloth will wrap around to the front cover. For this size book I find 1¼ in/32 mm is a pleasing balance between the bookcloth wrapping and the decorative paper. Measure that distance from the left and draw a pencil line from top to bottom on your cover. This will help you place your window. Continue to draw the pencil line around to the back of the cover as well. This will help you position the bookcloth when you're gluing your cover [A].

Note → There will be a bit of an optical illusion here with the distance from left to right between the actual width of the cover and the distance between the edge of the bookcloth and the right edge of the book. This is the reason for the next step.

2. Trim a piece of scrap paper to 2 × 2 in/51 × 51 mm. You will use this to position the window where you think it looks best. The one shown here is 3¼ in/83 mm from the bottom, 3 in/76 mm from the top, 2¾ in/70 mm from the fore-edge and 2¼ in/57 mm from the bookcloth edge [B].

3. Once you have placed the scrap paper where you like it, outline the square in pencil directly onto the board, then use your triangle ruler to redraw the lines against the straight edges of the cover [C].

4. Now you will trim out the window. I suggest standing for this step, as it will give you more leverage and be better for your shoulders. I also recommend using a fresh blade in your craft knife. Line up the triangle ruler at the edge of your cover on any side. Place the tip of your craft knife at the corner of the pencil border and begin slicing through the board.

Note → You will not be able to trim all the way through the bookboard in one go. Take it slowly. If you cut beyond your window, don't fret. As long as your corners are aligned, the window will pop out nicely and you can smooth out the extra cut line by burnishing with your bone folder [D].

5. Trim your spine for your cover by holding the interior spine piece up against the extra bookboard. Take into consideration the thickness of the backing of the screw-post – about an ⅛ in/3 mm. The front portion of the spine piece gets glued in close to the cover/hinge area on the front, so you don't need to compensate for any thickness there [E].

6. After you've measured and trimmed your cover spine, test the cut piece by holding it up against the interior spine piece with the front piece close to the edge to see how much room you have for the back [F].

A ↓

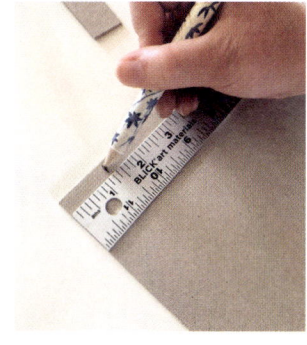

B ↓

C ↓

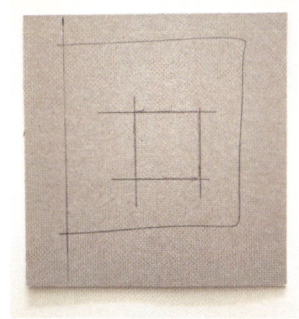

D ↓

E ↓

F ↓

Glue the cover ↓

1. First, be sure that your front cover, spine piece and back cover are oriented correctly. Place your bookcloth fabric side down, line up the edge of your front cover at the pencil line where the cloth will meet your decorative paper and draw your glue boundaries onto the bookcloth [A].

2. Place the hinge spacer up against the cover and place the spine up against the hinge spacer. Draw a pencil line around the spine.

3. Place the hinge spacer on the other side of the spine, place the back cover against the hinge spacer and draw a pencil line around the cover [B].

4. Position your bookcloth fabric side down onto a piece of scrap paper and begin to glue the area to the right of the spine, brushing your glue horizontally off the edge of the fabric. Remove the scrap paper after glueing [C].

5. Position your first cover piece on the glued fabric. Line up the pencil line on the back of your board with the edge of the bookcloth and press.

6. Glue your spine area, position your hinge spacer snugly up against your first cover piece and position your spine piece onto the bookcloth and up against the hinge spacer simultaneously and press [D].

7. Place a fresh piece of scrap paper under the unglued side of your bookcloth, brush a light layer of glue, position your hinge spacer snugly up against the spine, take your second cover piece and position it up against the hinge spacer and press. Again, be sure your covers and spines are aligned at the top. Flip your cover over onto its underside and smooth out the fabric with the bone folder.

8. Making sure there is no glue residue on your working surface, place your cover with the bookcloth side down. Place a piece of scrap paper under your cover, and swish a bit of glue

A ↓

B ↓

C ↓

D ↓

E ↓

F ↓

on your top and bottom bookcloth flaps. Move the gluey paper away from your surface.

9. Use the surface to mould the bookcloth around the edge of your bottom cover, then use your thumb and forefingers to smooth out the bookcloth to the inside [E].

10. Take your two pieces of Japanese decorative paper and draw glue boundaries before glueing. Place the paper decorative side down

and position your cover so the edge of the paper overlaps your fabric by ¼ in/6 mm, then draw around the three sides of your cover [F].

11. Position your back cover face down on your surface close to where you are glueing. Take a piece of scrap paper and place it under your first piece of decorative paper, glue inside and a little over the glue boundaries. Before lifting your paper off the surface, move your glueing paper aside, then lift up your glued decorative paper and position it on the back cover, lining it up to the edge of the bookcloth, overlapping by about ¼ in/6 mm. Once your paper is in place, press out any bubbles using your bone folder or the palm of your hand.

12. Take your hinge/corner spacer and place it up against the top corner at a 45° angle, draw a pencil line along the edge of the corner spacer, and use your craft knife to cut on the line. You can also cut directly along the corner spacer. Do the same for the opposite corner [G].

Note → Save all corner pieces as you will be using them later.

13. Next you will glue your top and bottom flaps simultaneously. Take a piece of scrap paper, place it under your top and bottom flaps, swish a smidgen of glue on your flaps and then use the surface to mould the paper around the cover, as you did for the bookcloth.

14. Swish a light layer of glue on your fore-edge flap, leaving a border at the edge so that the glue doesn't squish out when you press it. Crimp in the corners of the paper with your bone folder or fingertips, then mould the paper around the cover. This creates a lovely finish to your inside corners [H].

15. Glue your decorative paper to the front cover with the window [I].

G ↓

H ↓

I ↓

J ↓

K ↓

L ↓

16. Flip the cover over, being sure there's no glue on your surface, and use your craft knife to cut an 'X' in the window from corner to corner. Use your corner spacer at a 45° angle, and use your craft knife to cut along the edge [J].

17. Mould and press the flaps to the inside cover. Use your bone folder to smooth out the window edges [K].

18. Take your four corner pieces from Step 12 and glue them to the outside corners of the window edge on the interior on the cover [L].

Measure and punch the holes in the interior spine piece ↓

1. Take your three-hole punch and adjust the placement of the holes to your liking. (For reference, mine were 1 in/25 mm from the top, 1 in/25 mm from the bottom and 4 in/102 mm from the centre). Trim a piece of cover paper the same height as your pages and about 3 in/7.5 cm wide to use as a template. Punch the holes onto that first to test whether the holes are evenly placed.

2. Place your template onto the inside of the back interior spine piece. Use your pencil to outline the interior of the holes [A].

3. Punch holes onto this piece first using a mallet and your single hole punch [B].

4. Align the back of the spine piece to the inside of the front piece, then take your pencil and outline the interior of those holes. You will have hold it tight while you pencil in the outlines of the original holes [C].

5. Unfold it and place the front piece flat on the surface, then punch the holes onto the inside of the spine front piece [D].

A ↓

B ↓

C ↓

D ↓

Glue in the interior spine piece ↓

1. Place a piece of scrap paper on your working surface. Hold up the spine piece and glue the spine area only, then rest one of the flaps as close to the surface as possible and glue that flap. Rotate your spine piece so that you can glue the other flap [A].

> Note → The best way to hold up the spine piece while glueing is to put your forefinger between the two spine piece flaps while you hold it in the air and glue the spine. Glue in the centre, and then up and down off the edges. Don't use too much glue, or it will squish out.

A ↓

B ↓

C ↓

2. Position your spine piece gently and give yourself an aerial view to be sure it's evenly placed [B].

3. Smooth out the interior of the spine first. The Crescent board pieces will be upright at this point, but you'll still need to press them from the top so that they are attached securely. Use your Teflon bone folder to burnish the groove into the hinge area and then smooth out the flaps [C].

Glue in the interior panels ↓

1. Place your front cover interior decorative paper to the inside of the cover, being sure that there's an even border around the paper [A].

2. Use a bit of washi tape (or painter's tape) to keep the paper temporarily attached while you flip the cover over and draw a pencil line inside the window onto the back of the decorative paper. Remove the tape and place your paper flat onto the surface for trimming.

3. You will want a bit of a border around the opening of the interior window edge, so I suggest trimming the paper about ⅛ in/3 mm beyond your pencil border. If that's not enough, you can always trim away more. Draw an 'X' at the top of your paper to match the 'X' on your interior front cover so you'll know which is the top when you're glueing [B].

4. Glue in your back cover panel.

5. Glue your front cover panel, first glueing the sides of the paper, then glueing off the outer edges and then towards the window edge. Lift the sheet and hover it over the front cover, giving yourself an aerial view. Gently place the paper onto the cover while making sure that the edges of the window are evenly placed. Smooth/burnish with your Teflon bone folder [C].

6. Press under a weight for at least an hour.

A ↓

B ↓

C ↓

Prepare pages for binding ↓

1. Score your pages 1 in/25 mm from the left margin [A].

2. Punch the holes in your pages using your three-hole punch using the same hole placement as on your interior spine piece [B].

3. Insert your screws, add the pages, close the back spine piece, and attach the screw-backings [C+D].

A blush of accomplishment ensues!

A ↓

B ↓

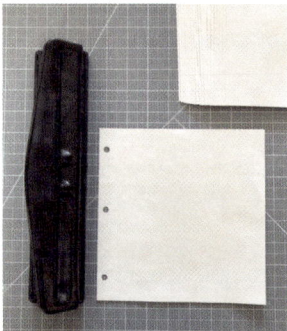

C ↓

D ↓

8

LONG-STITCH-LINK-STITCH ALBUM

WITH HAND-FOLDED ENVELOPES

WHAT YOU'LL MAKE

A beautiful and useful ephemera album or travel diary with hard covers and a soft fabric spine, and a pair of bound-in hand-folded envelopes with string-and-button closure. The album measures 5½ × 7½ × 1¼ in/140 × 191 × 32 mm.

Skill Level → ● ● ● ● ○

Materials ↓

- 2 pieces of bookboard cut to cover size (5½ × 7½ in/140 × 191 mm)
- 1½ sheets of Stonehenge 250 gsm paper (parent sheet 22 × 30 in/559 × 762 mm)
- 2 pieces of bookcloth
    - 1 outer spine piece (3⅜ × 9 in/86 × 229 mm)
    - 1 inner spine piece (3½ × 7¼ in/89 × 184 mm)
- 2 pieces of Carta Varese decorative paper for your front and back cover (6 × 9 in/152 × 229 mm)
- 2 pieces of Stonehenge for your interior cover (5¼ × 7¼ in/133 × 184 mm)
- 2 sheets of Hahnemühle Bugra for your paper sandwich (10 × 13 in/254 × 330 mm)
- 2 sheets of Grafix Double Tack for your paper sandwich (10 × 13 in/254 × 330 mm)
- 2 sheets of Carta Varese decorative paper for your paper sandwich (10 × 13 in/254 × 330 mm)
- 3 lengths of 4-ply waxed linen thread in different colours
    - 1 length measuring 3 yd/2.75 m (for stitching)
    - 2 lengths measuring 10 in/255 mm (for the buttons)
- 4 beautiful buttons (½–¾ in/12–19 mm)
- 1 hinge and corner spacer (2 pieces of bookboard (1 × 5 in/254 × 127 mm) the same thickness as your cover, glued together)

Tools ↓

- bone folder
- Teflon bone folder
- shipping clerk's knife
- craft knife
- metal ruler
- triangle ruler
- lightweight awl
- medium awl
- size 18 bookbinding needle
- PVA glue
- glue brush
- a cup for your glue
- scrap paper for glueing on
- a small cloth to keep your fingers glue free
- washi tape
- pencil
- scissors
- scallop shears (optional)
- cutting mat
- double-adhesive tape
- a cloth-covered brick or heavy weight for pressing your covers

Fold the signatures and make the envelopes ↓

1. Follow Steps 1–3 of **Folding signatures** (see **Techniques**, p.20). You now have four sheets, each measuring 11 × 15 in/279 × 381 mm.

2. Take one of your four pieces, fold it in half and slice again [A].

3. Use your working surface to line up the bottom edges. Use your bone folder to fold them in half, then set aside [B].

4. Repeat with the other pieces until you have three 4-page signatures.

> Note → There's no need to press your signatures after folding. The puffier the signatures, the more room you'll have in your book for adding collage, photos, or bits of ephemera.

5. Follow Steps 1–3 of **Making a paper sandwich** (see **Techniques**, p.21), using the two sheets of Hahnemühle Bugra [C+D].

A ↓

B ↓

C ↓

D ↓

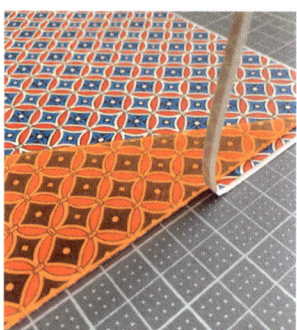

Hand-fold the two inner envelopes and attach the buttons ↓

1. Position your paper sandwich horizontally.

2. Take your ruler and measure 4 in/102 mm from the right (which will be your bottom flap). Line up your triangle ruler at the 4 in/102 mm mark and use your bone folder to score the sheet. Fold at the score line and crease with your bone folder, then open and press flat [A].

3. Measure the width of your signature and make a note of it. Mine was 5½ in/139 mm. Use your ruler and triangle ruler to measure that distance up from your first score line and score to create the body of your envelope. Decide if you'd like your top flap to be deep or

shallow, then trim accordingly. You will need to have an overlap of least 1 in/25 mm [B].

4. Position your paper sandwich vertically. Use your ruler and triangle ruler to measure 1 in/25 mm in from the right side. Measure at the top and bottom of the sheet to ensure that your side flap will be even, then score with your bone folder. Fold at the score line and burnish with your bone folder.

5. Measure the height of your signature – you will use this measurement to finish making the body of your envelope. Use your ruler and triangle ruler in tandem to measure the distance between your first side score line and

A ↓

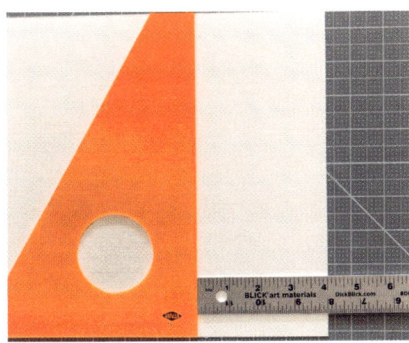

B ↓

C ↓

what will be your second. Measure your sheet at the top and bottom to ensure the space between the score lines is even, then score with your bone folder. Fold at the score line and burnish with your bone folder [C].

6. Trim your left flap to 1 in/25 mm to match the flap on the other side.

Trim the envelope corners ↓

1. Beginning at the bottom right corner, make a pencil mark ⅛ in/3 mm to the left of the score line. Then make your way to the bottom left corner, make a pencil mark ⅛ in/3 mm to the right of the score line. Rotate your paper clockwise by 90° and repeat around the sheet. Note the ½ in/13 mm measurement at the top of the side flaps [A].

2. Starting again at the bottom right corner, place the tip of your pencil in the intersection of the score lines, place your triangle ruler up against your pencil, line it up with the pencil mark at the edge of your sheet and draw a line. Repeat around the sheet.

3. Slice away the corners across the pencil lines. Keep the corner pieces. You will use these to make paper patches for the back of your envelope flaps [B].

4. Repeat for the other envelope [C].

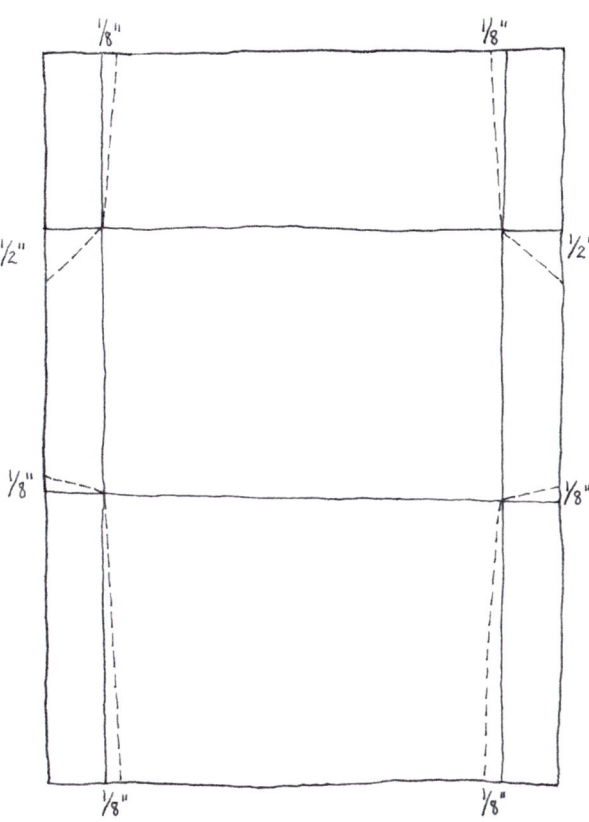

A ↓

B ↓

C ↓

Note → You can pencil these trimming directions directly onto your paper sandwich. In my workshops I often suggest that students make up a template from cartridge paper for practice.

Attach buttons to the interior envelope and prepare the envelope for stitching ↓

1. Place one button on the top flap and one on the bottom flap in your preferred position. Once you have them spaced as you want them, take your metal ruler and measure either side to confirm that they are evenly placed horizontally [A].

2. Take a freshly sharpened pencil and make a pencil dot through the two buttonholes onto your envelope flaps [B].

3. Take your lightweight awl and pierce through the pencil marks [C].

4. Measure off two pieces of waxed linen thread 6 in/15 cm each. Thread through each of the buttons from the top and attach them through the top and bottom flaps of your envelope [D].

Repeat Steps 1–4 for your second envelope.

A ↓

B ↓

C ↓

D ↓

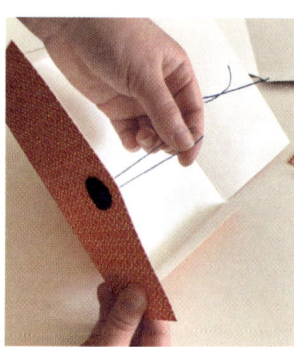

E ↓

F ↓

G ↓

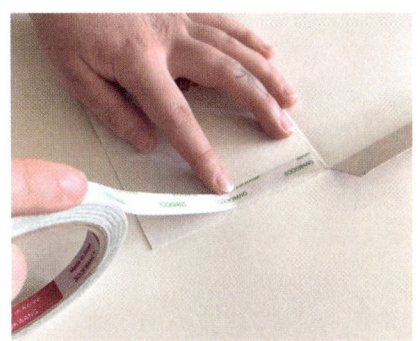

5. Follow Steps 1–2 from **Covering button knots** (see **Techniques**, p.22) using four corners from the trimmed paper sandwich [E+F].

6. Trim two pieces of double-adhesive tape to the height of your bottom flap. See [G] for placement.

7. If you prefer to use a glue stick you'll apply the glue in the same area once you've finished stitching your booklet and hand-folding your presentation envelope. You will seal your envelopes after you've finished stitching.

Make the cover ↓

1. Take two pieces of bookboard and make a pencil mark 1 in/25 mm from the edge at both the top and bottom. Place your bookcloth fabric side down and position your first cover piece on top, lining up the edge of the cloth with the pencil marks on your cover [A].

2. Use a pencil to draw around the edge of the bookboard onto the bookcloth. Then place your second cover, leaving a 1¼ in/32 mm space between the two, and draw a pencil line around that piece. Set the covers aside [B].

3. Take a piece of scrap paper and place it under the bookcloth. Apply an even swish of glue down your right-hand glue boundary and then brush the glue horizontally off the edges, smoothing out your glue ridges. Remove the scrap paper, then place your first cover piece onto the glued bookcloth and press [C].

4. Rotate your cover and glue the other side of the bookcloth, then gently position your second cover piece inside the pencil lines.

Before you press, take your ruler and confirm the width of your spine is even at the top and bottom at 1¼ in/32 mm. Use a ruler or any straight edge to make sure the two cover pieces are aligned at the bottom. Press down [D].

5. Make sure there is no glue on your working surface and flip your cover fabric side up and smooth out any bubbles under your bookcloth.

6. Position your cover fabric side down again and place a piece of scrap paper under the top and bottom turn-ins.

7. Lightly swish some glue on both ends then lift the cover, remove the gluey paper and use the surface to mould the turn-ins around the edge of the top and bottom. Use your Teflon bone folder or thumbs and forefingers and press the turn-ins down [E].

B ↓

E ↓

C ↓

D ↓

Glue your decorative papers to the front and back covers ↓

> Note → Your decorative paper will overlap your bookcloth by ⅛ in/3 mm. It's fine if it overlaps a smidgen more, but ⅛ in/3 mm is my minimum.

1. Take both of your cover papers and draw your glue boundaries [A].

2. Place one of your decorative papers pattern side down with a piece of scrap paper underneath and brush on a light layer of glue – it's fine to go a little over the pencil lines. Remove the gluey paper, then lift your paper with both hands and suspend it over the cover to give yourself an aerial view, then gently position the paper ⅛ in/3 mm over the bookcloth spine. Press and smooth out any bubbles [B].

3. Place your cover face up on the working surface. Deploy your corner spacer and place it up against the top corner at a 45° angle. Draw a pencil line. Do the same on the bottom corner, then use your craft knife (or scissors, if that's more comfortable) to trim along the pencil line [C].

4. First, you will glue down your top and bottom flaps. Begin by placing a piece of scrap paper under your top and bottom flaps. Swish a light layer of glue, and then move the gluey paper aside and lift your cover up, using the surface to mould one side around your bookboard (as you did with the bookcloth spine), then reverse the cover and repeat. While you're pressing one side onto the surface, use your fingers and thumbs to secure the flap, then flip the cover around and finish the other side in the same way [D].

A ↓

B ↓

5. Place a piece of scrap paper under your side flap, brush a light swish of glue, then remove the scrap paper.

C ↓

D ↓

6. Crimp the nooks. I prefer to use my fingernails for this part because I can feel the paper and the edges and corner of the boards, but you can use the tip of your bone folder if you like [E].

7. Use the working surface to mould the turn-in around the edge of the cover. Use your fingers to smooth over the turn-in to the inside of the cover [F].

Repeat Steps 2–7 for your back cover.

E ↓

F ↓

Finish the interior of the cover ↓

1. Take your interior spine bookcloth and double check that the height is ¼ in/6 mm less than the height of your cover, and wide enough to give you at least 1 in/25 mm of bookcloth on the inside of the covers [A].

2. Begin with a light swish of glue in the centre and brush out on all four edges, especially the top and bottom because these will be seen. Give yourself an aerial view and place the bookcloth down so that there's an ⅛ in/3 mm border at the top and bottom [B].

A ↓

3. Trim two pieces of Stonehenge paper for the front and back interior panels. Leave a border of at least ⅛ in/3 mm all around [C].

4. Glue both front and back interior panels. All four edges will be seen, so the best way to glue these two pieces is to start in the centre and glue out in a star pattern, so that you are glueing off the edge on all four sides.

5. Press your cover for at least half an hour. If your cover continues to bow, press it for longer.

Create your stitching template ↓

1. Trim a piece of Stonehenge to fit snugly inside the width and height of your spine, 1⅛ × 7½ in/28 × 190 mm. Your finished template will have five vertical and six horizontal stitching rows.

2. Place your template vertically and draw a pencil line down the centre from top to bottom. Draw four additional lines, two to the right and two to the left of the centre, ³⁄₁₆ in/5 mm apart. That should leave you with a space of at least ⅛ in/3 mm on each side of the first and last stitching row [A].

3. Turn your template so that it is horizontal. First, measure ½ in/51 mm from each end and use your triangle ruler to draw your pencil lines [B].

4. Measure 1 in/25 mm in from each end and make a line there, then make another 1¾ in/44 mm towards the centre from those [C].

5. Make a little pencil dot at each of the intersections, and using your medium awl and straight edge to make sure the stations are aligned, pierce holes in your template. Repeat with your lightweight awl to open the holes a smidgen more [D].

B ↓

C ↓

A ↓
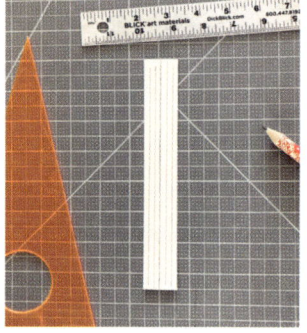

B ↓

C ↓

D ↓

Note → When marking up your signatures and envelopes you may also need a white pencil or dark marker so that you'll be able to see the dots on the folds. You can also use a hard graphite pencil and make more of an indentation.

Transfer stitching stations ↓

1. Use a bit of washi tape or masking tape to securely position the template. Keeping the cover flat on the surface, use your medium awl to pierce through each of the sewing stations, then remove the template and pierce though each station with your lightweight awl to widen them [A].

2. Arrange signatures and envelopes as you prefer, with the envelope tops facing up so that they face out when open [B].

3. Take your last signature (or envelope) and line it up with the last sewing station. Make a pencil mark at each of the stations. Repeat this step with each of the four signatures/envelopes, from back to front [C].

4. Pierce the sewing stations with your lightweight awl and you are now ready to begin stitching [D]!

A ↓

B ↓

C ↓

D ↓

Stitch the book ↓

Measure a length of thread 12 times the height of your book. This will give you enough for tying off your ends easily, and a little extra. You will also need an extra piece of thread 2 in/5 cm long … you will see why!

You will be stitching your book from back to front, so when I say refer to your first signature, I mean the one that will be placed last in the book.

1. Thread your needle, take your first envelope (or signature), open it and exit through station 5 of both your signature and cover. Pull the thread through and leave a 5 in/12.5 cm tail on the inside [A].

↑ This technique always requires an even number of stitching rows, but the actual stitching steps remain the same no matter the pattern you design (as shown here in the stitching variations).

2. Enter station 4 (signature and cover). Exit station 3.

3. Enter station 2. Exit station 1 [B].

4. Now your thread is on the outside of the book at the top. Go back into station 1 and pull the thread all the way through, leaving a little loop on the spine [C].

5. Then slide your separate 2 in/5 cm piece of thread through the loop and tie a gentle half knot around the loop to keep it from pulling through while you stitch back down through the same signature [D].

6. Begin stitching back down, following your previous stitches. Exit station 2 in row 5.

7. Enter station 3. Exit station 4.

8. Enter station 5 through the cover only. Your thread will come out on the inside of the spine, and you'll be making a slightly angled stitch on the inside of the spine [E].

9. Exit through station 6 of the cover in row 2, without the signature.

10. Enter station 6 in row 1 and tie off at station 6 [F+G]. Exit station 6 in row 5 [H].

11. Enter station 6 in row 4 and bring in the next signature [I]. Exit station 5 in row 2.

12. Enter station 4. Exit station 3.

13. Enter station 2. Exit station 1.

14. Take your needle and come through the loop in row 1 (remove the small piece of thread) pull your thread through and enter station 1 of row 4 [J]. Exit station 2 in row 4.

15. Enter station 3. Exit station 4.

A ↓ B ↓ C ↓ D ↓

E ↓ F ↓ G ↓ H ↓

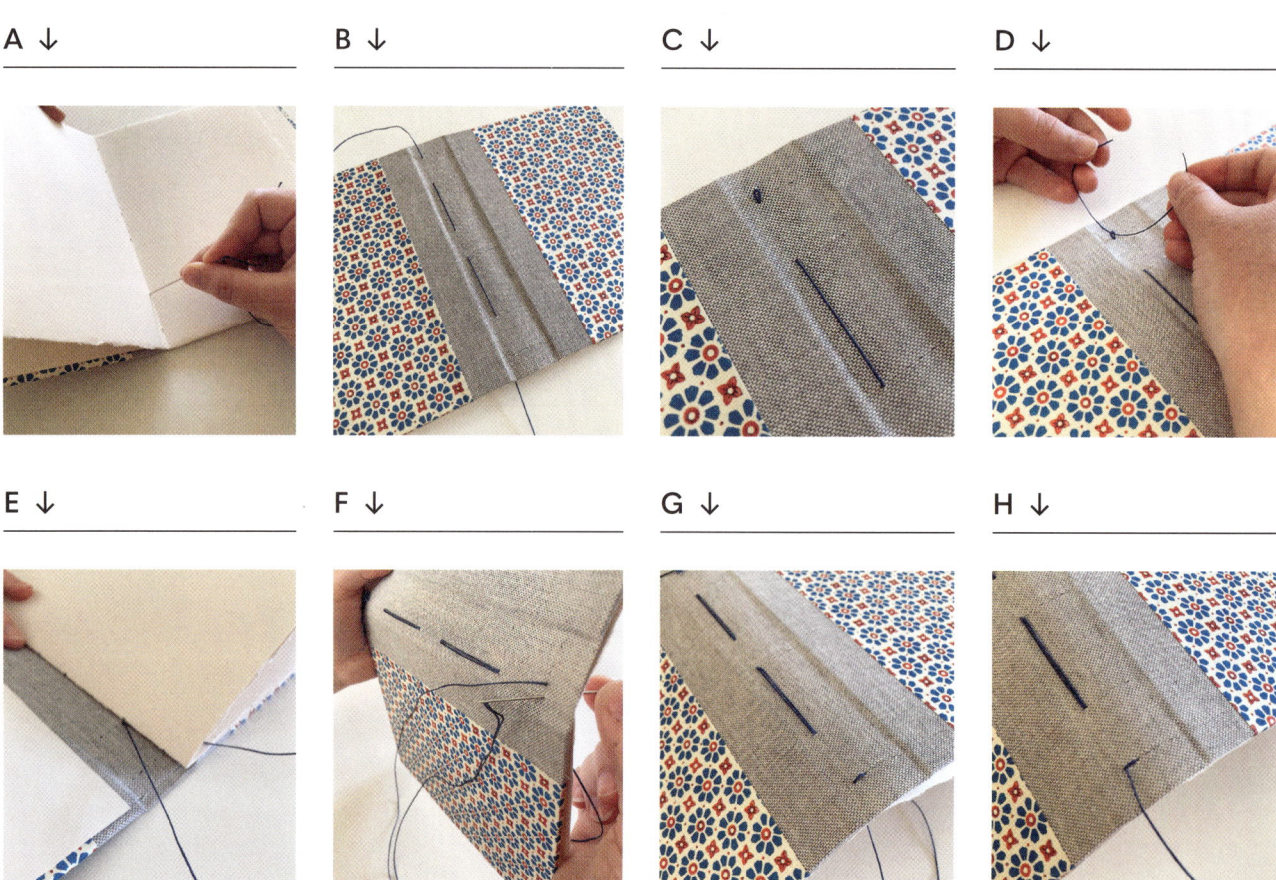

16. Enter station 5 through the spine of the cover only [K]. Exit station 6 in row 3 [L].

17. Come through the loop at the top in row 2 [M].

18. Enter station 6 in row 3 and bring in the next signature [N].

19. Keep calm and carry on stitching! If using two lengths of thread, attach your second length of thread with a weaver's knot or a double knot when needed (see **Techniques**, p.23). When you get to row 1 you will enter station 5 through both the cover and signature, and will tie off right there [O]!

I ↓

J ↓

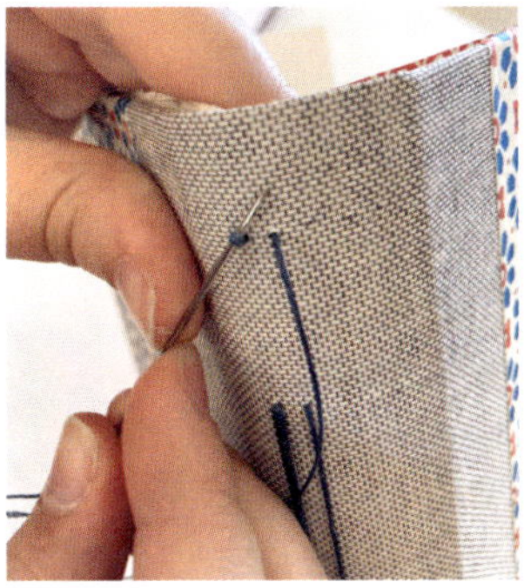

K ↓

L ↓

M ↓

N ↓

O ↓

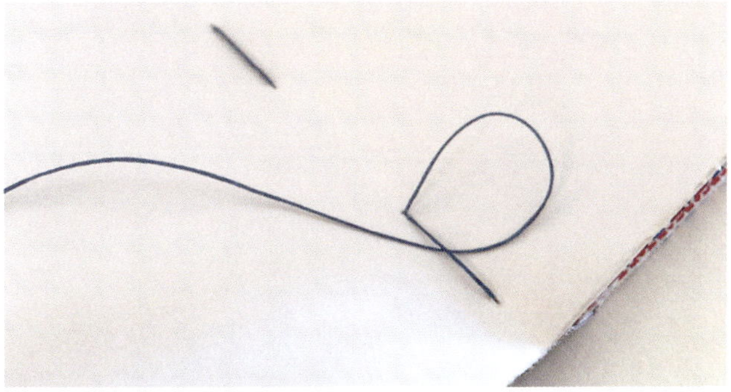

Seal your bottom envelope flaps and attach closing thread ↓

1. Expose the strips of adhesive on your bottom envelope flaps. Seal and press.

2. Measure a length of thread that will wind around both buttons a couple of times, plus a few extra inches/cm. Wrap the thread around one button, tie a double knot. You can also press the button to flatten the bulkiness of the thread knot.

Repeat Steps 1–2 for the other envelope.

A blush of accomplishment ensues!

09

TRIPTYCH OF COPTIC-STITCH BINDINGS

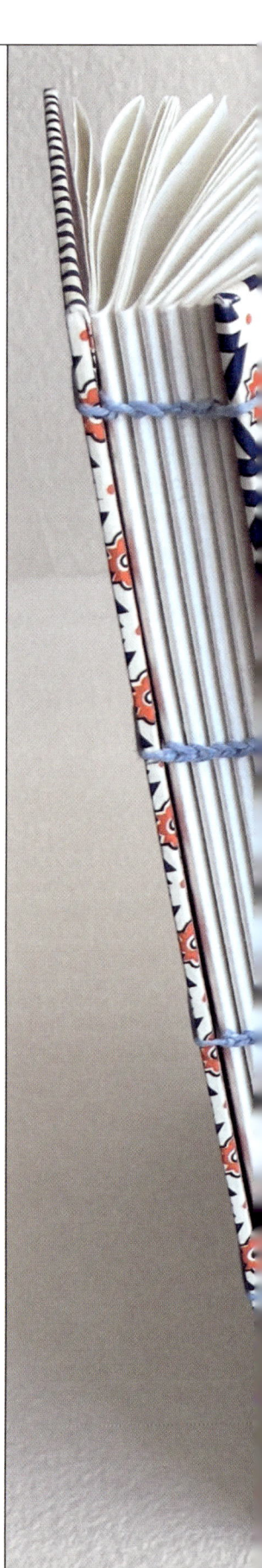

WHAT YOU'LL MAKE

Three books using different styles of Coptic-stitch binding. The traditional hardcover binding uses one curved needle, the multi-needle hardcover binding uses four curved needles, and the softcover binding uses one curved needle. All three of your books will measure 8½ × 5½ × 1 in/216 × 140 × 25 mm, each with 48 pages/96 serendipitous sides, with deckled edges on the top, bottom and fore-edge of each page.

Tools ↓

- bone folder
- Teflon bone folder
- shipping clerk's knife
- craft knife
- metal ruler
- triangle ruler
- lightweight awl
- medium awl
- 4 curved needles
- PVA glue
- glue brush

- a cup for your glue
- scrap paper for glueing on
- a small cloth to keep your fingers glue free
- pencil
- scissors
- cutting mat
- washi tape
- a cloth-covered brick or heavy weight for pressing
- 1 corner spacer

Using a curved needle →
The actual style of the Coptic stitch requires the thread to wrap behind each stitch that connects the signatures and covers. Using a curved needle simply makes it easier to stitch in this style.

A note about the Coptic stitch →
You will notice in my directions that I always suggest you wrap your curved needle behind the stitch from left to right, whether or not you're stitching the current signature from right to left or left to right. The reason I do this, and suggest you do the same, is that your stitches will look more even and consistent overall. If you find it more comfortable to wrap around the stitch from right to left, that's absolutely OK, whichever you decide keep it consistent and your stitching will look more refined.

SOFTCOVER BOOK

Materials ↓

- 2 sheets of Judd Street 90 gsm paper trimmed to size (12 × 16 in/305 × 406 mm)
- 2 sheets of Grafix Double Tack for your softcover paper sandwich
  (11 × 14 in/254 × 330 mm)
- 2 sheets of Stonehenge 250 gsm paper (12 × 16 in/305 × 406 mm)
- 1½ sheets of Hahnemühle Bugra paper (31½ × 44¾ in/800 × 1137 mm)
- 2 pieces of heavy cardstock for reinforcing your soft covers
  (8¼ × 11 in/210 × 279 mm)
- 1 length of waxed linen thread (3 yd/2.75 m each)
- 6 strips of double-adhesive tape (¼ × 8 in/6 × 203 mm)
- 2 nickel-plated paper clips or bulldog clips

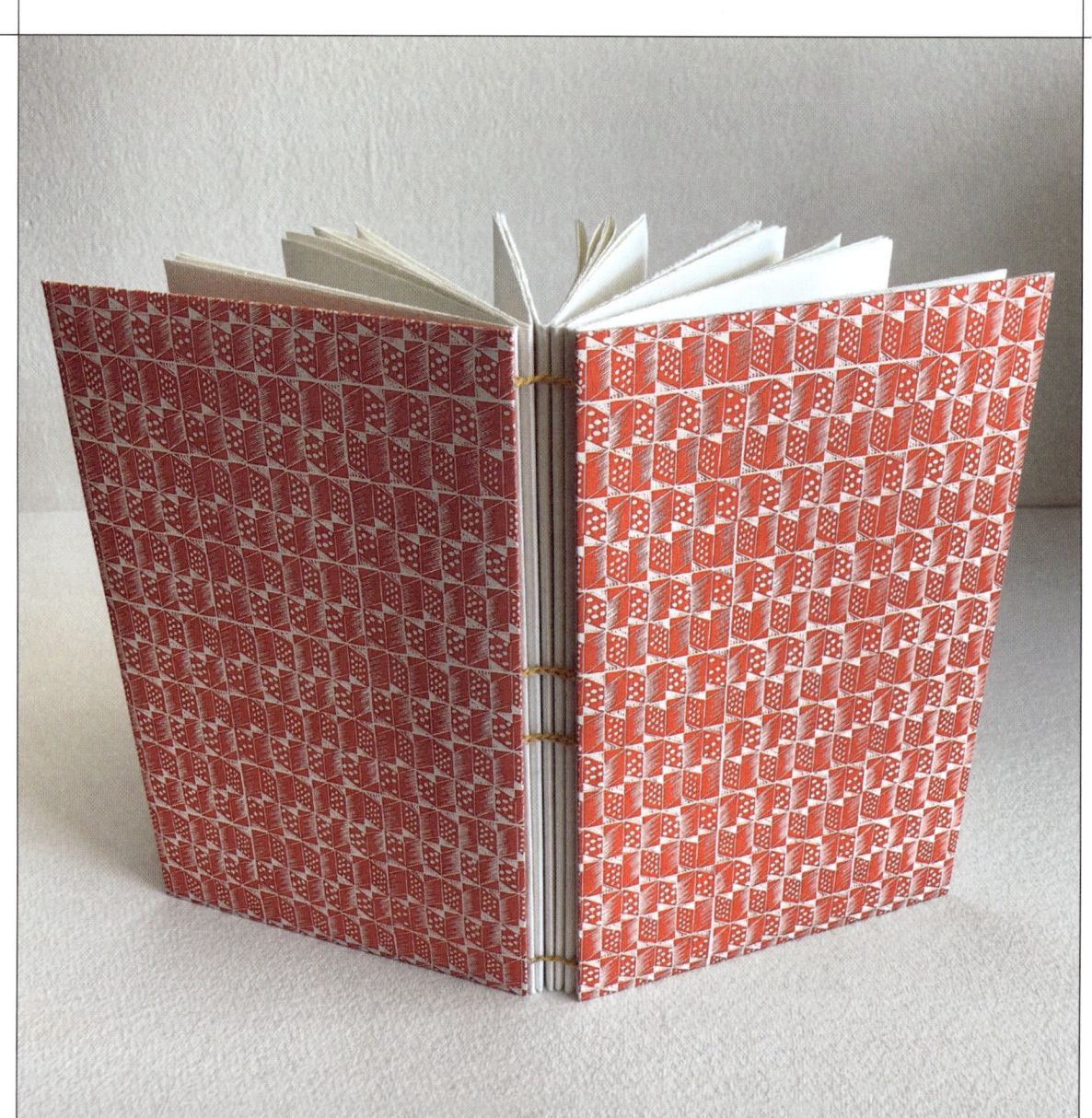

Fold the signatures ↓

Follow Steps 1–3 of **Folding signatures** (see **Techniques**, p.20) using one of your sheets of Hahnemühle Bugra. You now have four smaller pieces measuring 16¾ × 20⁶/₇ in/42.5 × 52.9 cm.

Repeat with your three remaining full-sized sheets, creating 12 pieces measuring 16¾ × 20⁶/₇ in/42.5 × 52.9 cm.

Note → In the following steps you will fold these sheets to create a total of 20 signatures (or 18 if you prefer to keep the extra two unfolded).

A ↓   B ↓

1. Take one quarter sheet (16¾ × 20⁶/₇ in/42.5 × 52.9 cm), fold it in half with your bone folder and slice it with your shipping clerk's knife. Use your working surface to line up the bottom edges, fold the two sheets together and slice with your shipping clerk's knife [A].

2. Line up the bottom edges as before, fold gently, lining the corners up on the left, and use your bone folder to fold them into your first 8-page signature. Set it aside and repeat until you have a lovely stack of 18 signatures [B].

Make the paper sandwich for your softcovers ↓

Make two paper sandwiches. Follow Steps 1–3 of **Making a paper sandwich** (see **Techniques**, p.21) using your two sheets of Stonehenge for the backing paper, and Judd Street papers (12 × 16 in/305 × 406 mm) for the decorative paper.

Prepare the paper sandwich for stitching ↓

Note → Follow my scoring tips (see **Techniques**, p.22) if your triangle ruler isn't long enough for the length of the cover.

1. Position your paper sandwich horizontally, decorative side down.

2. Place the straight edge of your triangle ruler 1 in/25 mm from the right edge and use your ruler to confirm this measurement is exactly the same at the top and bottom, then score with the tip of your bone folder. Fold over at the score line, crease with your bone folder, then open and flatten. This first fold is your spine score, which I will refer to as we make our way around the cover scoring and trimming [A].

3. Rotate your paper sandwich 90° so the spine fold is at the top. Centre a single signature up against the spine score. Hold the spine flap upright as you nestle the signature into the spine score [B].

4. Place your triangle ruler up against the signature on the left, then set the signature aside and use your bone folder to score. Fold over at the score line, crease with your bone folder, then open and flatten [C].

5. Rotate your cover 180° so that the spine score is at the bottom and your first side score is on the right. Measure the height of your signature, then nestle it into the spine score and the side score so that it's perfectly aligned. Place the long end of your triangle ruler up against the signature, then set the signature aside [D].

6. Adjust the triangle ruler to give yourself a smidgen more than the height of your signature. Be sure to measure at both the top and bottom to confirm the distance is precise.

Note → I use the technique in Step 5 to get the triangle ruler into place, but I still adjust the ruler to be sure the distance from the first side score line to the second is correct. Optionally, after you get the triangle ruler into place you can make a pencil mark at the top and bottom of the triangle ruler and use those marks to guide you for scoring. This also makes it easier to realign your triangle ruler if it gets out of place.

7. Now you will make the fourth and final score line for the fore-edge. Measure the width of your signature and add ¼ in/6 mm. Using the long end of your triangle ruler, measure from the spine score line at both the top and bottom, then score. Fold over at the score line and crease with your bone folder, then open and flatten [E+F].

A ↓

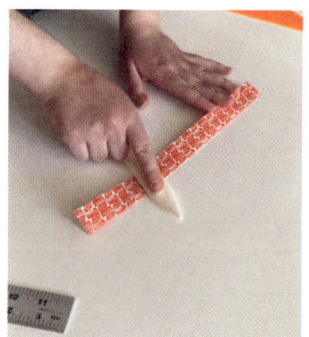

B ↓

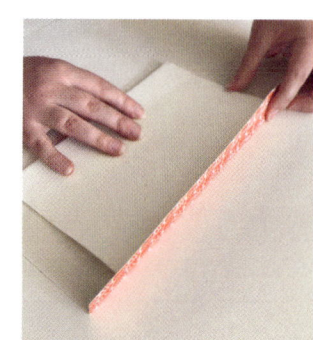

C ↓

D ↓

E ↓

F ↓

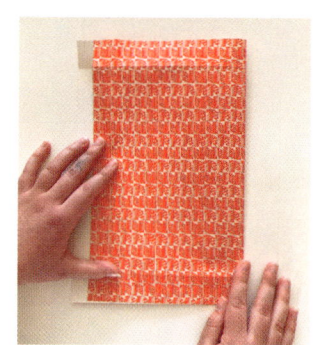

Repeat Steps 1–7 for your other cover.

Trim the softcovers ↓

1. Position your cover vertically. Make a pencil mark ¼ in/6 mm to the left of the score line on the right. Move clockwise from there around the cover, making pencil marks every ¼ in/6 mm. Do this on both covers [A].

2. Close the cover at the fore-edge with the spine flap folded and the extra flap facing up. Place your triangle ruler up against the spine and draw a pencil line [B].

3. Rotate the cover 180° and line up your triangle ruler ⅛ in/3 mm to the left of the pencil line, then trim the excess with your craft knife [C].

Repeat Steps 1–3 for your other cover.

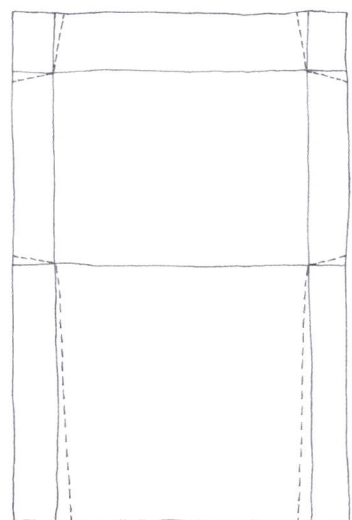

A ↓

B ↓

C ↓

Prepare the spines for stitching ↓

The softcover book requires an even number of sewing stations – for this project we will use four. The end stitches ('S' stitches) are placed at least ½ in/13 mm from the top and bottom of your spine. The two stations in the middle can be close to the end stitches or in the middle, whichever you prefer, although I suggest that you space them at a minimum of 1 in/25 mm for ease of stitching, especially if this is your first time making a Coptic-stitch book.

Assemble the softcovers ↓

Note → When you fold in all four flaps of your softcovers, it's good to secure them with a nickel-plated paper clip, or bulldog clip, to keep the cover closed while you are stitching.

1. First fold the spine flap in, followed by the two top and bottom flaps, then your fore-edge, then attach your clips. Repeat this step with your other cover [A+B].

2. Place your signatures between your covers so that the spine score flap (1 in/25 mm) is on the same side as the folds of your signature. When sandwiched together, the covers are positioned as here [C].

3. Jog your book on its spine and bottom edge to be sure your book is squared. Place it flat on your surface and place a book or heavy weight atop, about an inch/2.5 cm away from the spine [D].

A ↓

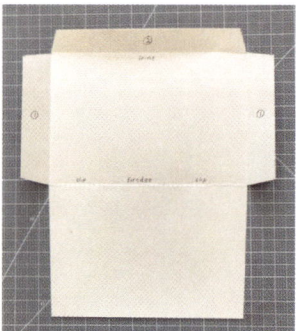

B ↓

C ↓

D ↓

Mark the sewing stations ↓

Note → It's always good to reconfirm your book has remained squared on the spine and bottom edge before marking your sewing stations. I like to do this by placing my triangle ruler up against the bottom edge and using the tips of your fingers to press the book into the flat surface of the triangle ruler [A].

1. Place your ruler flat on the surface in front of your book ½ in/13 mm from the right and position your triangle ruler up against the spine [B].

2. Take your pencil and run it up along the spine against the triangle ruler, making a little pencil mark on each of the signatures and the covers.

Repeat Steps 1 and 2 on the left.

3. Decide where you'd like to place your two additional sewing stations and measure accordingly. Then use your ruler, triangle ruler and pencil to mark each of the signatures and covers as you did for your end stations. My measurements are as in the illustration opposite.

A ↓   **B** ↓

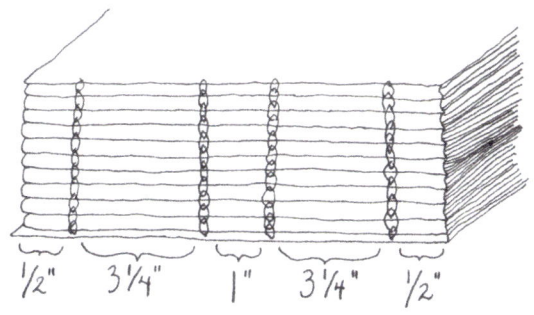

½" 3¼" 1" 3¼" ½"

Pierce the sewing stations and cover ↓

> Note → I suggest piercing stations 1 and 2 first, then rotating your signature to finish piercing stations 3 and 4. By rotating the signature, you will be less likely to crunch or crease your paper. You'll also have better leverage while piercing the lower stations.

1. Position your bookblock just to the side of your surface with the folds facing you. Begin with the top cover, open the spine flap and pierce the top two sewing stations. Then rotate your cover and pierce stations 3 and 4 [A].

2. Place the cover frontside down with the spine fold facing away from you and begin piercing the stations in your signatures and back cover in the same manner.

3. Place the first signature with the fold facing away from you to the other side of your work surface and repeat the same steps for the remaining signatures [B].

4. Place adhesive strips on the interior flaps of your cover. You will not seal your covers until you have finished stitching.

A ↓   **B** ↓

Stitch your softcover book ↓

1. Measure a piece of thread approximately eight times the height of your book (six signatures + two covers). Tie a half knot 1 in/25 mm from the tail of your thread. This keeps the tail from slipping out while you are stitching on your cover and first signature [A].

2. Position your book with the folds of the signature facing you. Set the top cover aside and bring in your first (top) signature. Begin in station 1 on the left.

3. Exit station 1 of the cover, pull the thread through till it reaches the half knot [B].

4. Enter station 1 of the signature [C]. Exit station 2 of the signature [D].

5. Enter station 2 of the cover [E]. Exit station 3 of the cover [F].

6. Enter station 3 of the signature [G]. Exit station 4 of the signature [H].

7. Enter station 4 of the cover [I]. Exit station 3 of the cover [J].

8. Enter station 3 of the signature [K]. Exit station 2 of the signature. Come out above the previous stitch [L].

9. Enter station 2 of the cover [M]. Exit station 1 of the cover [N].

10. Come from behind the stitch from left to right and pull the thread all the way through [O].

A ↓

B ↓

C ↓

D ↓

E ↓

F ↓

G ↓

H ↓

I ↓

J ↓

K ↓

L ↓

11. Turn your book over so the cover is on its back and the first signature is facing up. Bring in signature 2 [P].

12. Enter station 1 of the second signature [Q]. Exit station 2 [R].

13. Now you'll begin wrapping around stitching.

14. Wrap your needle behind the stitch from right to left then enter station 2 [S–U]. Exit station 3 [V].

15. Wrap behind the stitch then enter station 3 [W+X]. Exit station 4 [Y].

16. Here's where you will make your first S-stitch. Wrap your needle around the stitch from right to left (cover and first signature) [Z].

17. Pull the thread all the way through but leave a little loop. Come through the loop and pull up and tighten gently [AA+BB].

18. Bring in signature 3. Enter station 4 [CC]. Exit station 3 [DD].

19. Wrap around stitch, enter station 3 [EE]. Exit station 2 and wrap around [FF].

20. Enter station 2 [GG]. Exit station 1, make an S-stitch and bring in signature 4 [HH].

> Note → If you used two shorter lengths of thread, here's where you may need to join the second length with either a weaver's knot or a double knot (see **Techniques**, p.23). I recommend joining it in one of the middle signatures if possible.

Continue stitching the remainder of signatures and cover in the same manner. After your final S-stitch in station 6, you will stitch on your front cover as if it were a signature and tie off inside the front cover [II+JJ].

M ↓

N ↓

O ↓

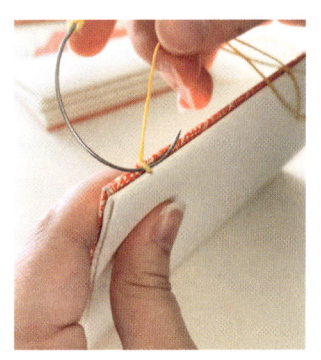

P ↓

Q ↓

R ↓

S ↓

T ↓

U ↓

V ↓

W ↓

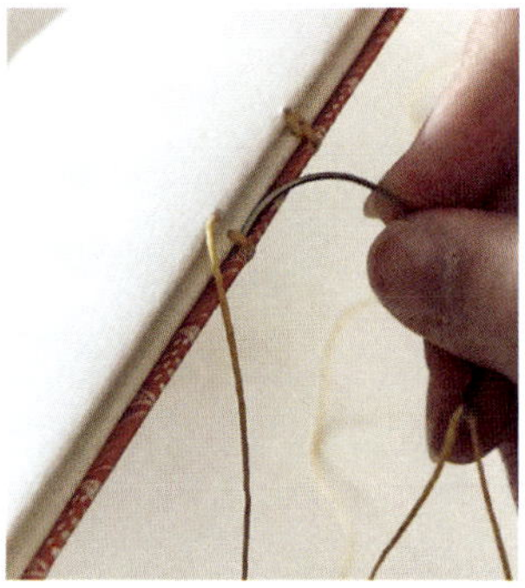

X ↓

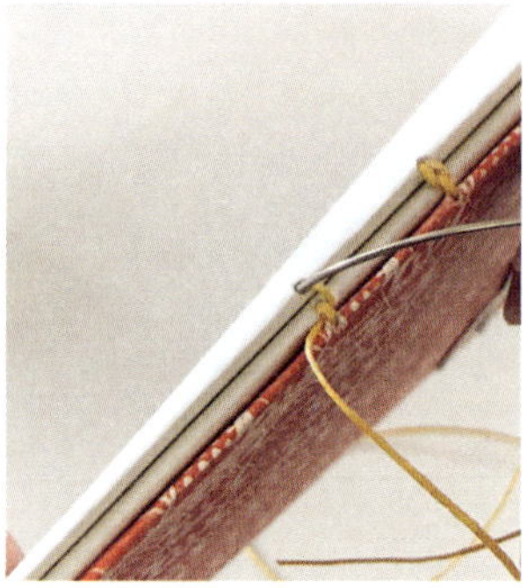

Y ↓

Z ↓

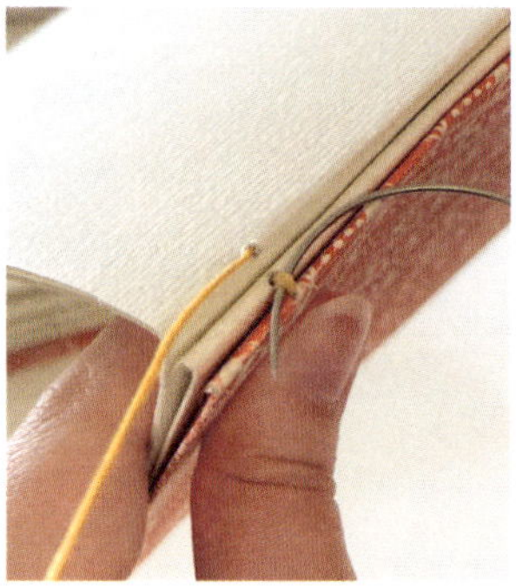

AA ↓

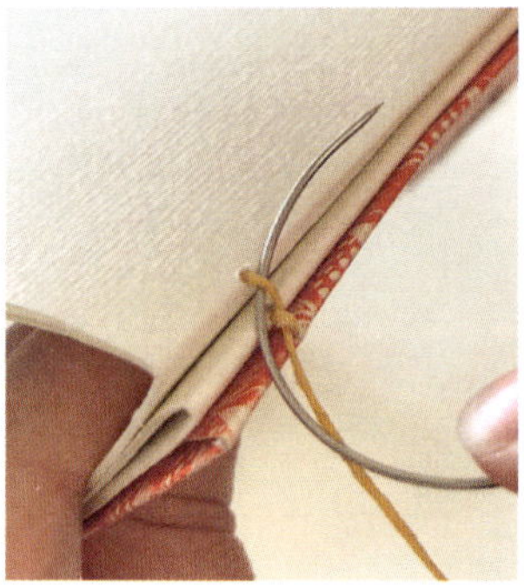

BB ↓

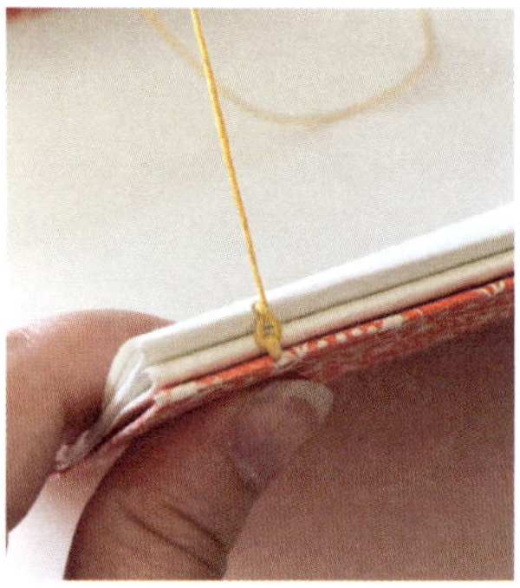

CC ↓

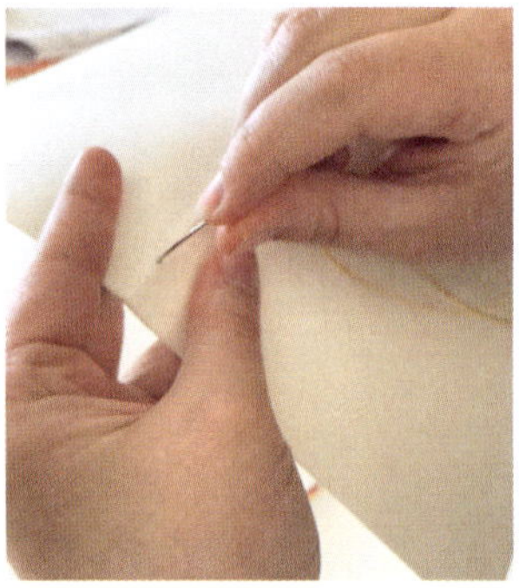

DD ↓

EE ↓

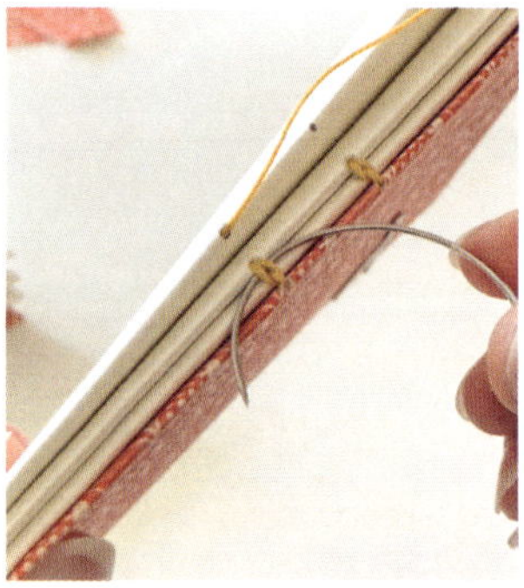

FF ↓

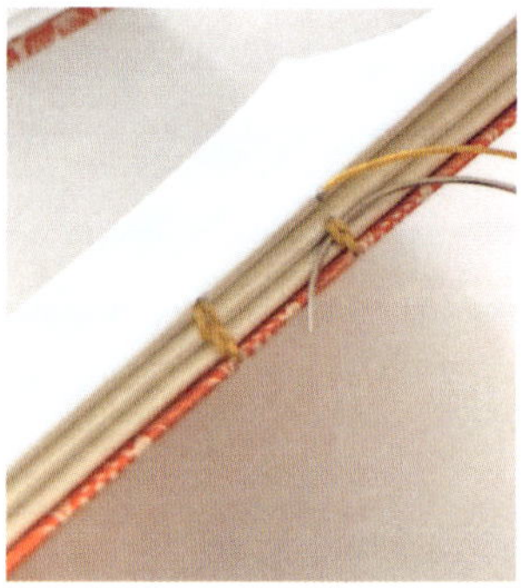

GG ↓

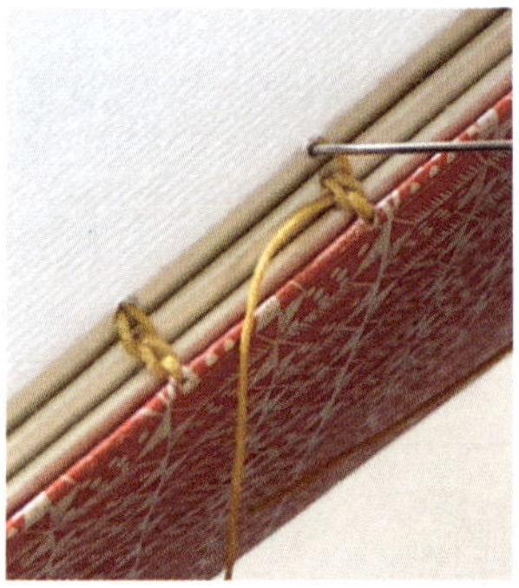

HH ↓

II ↓

JJ ↓

Finish the cover ↓

1. Take your two pieces of Stonehenge (8½ × 11 in/216 × 279 mm) and fold them in half.

2. Expose the double-adhesive strips on one cover and place one folded piece of Stonehenge inside the cover [A].

3. Place the folded Stonehenge inside the body of the cover [B].

4. Fold your top and bottom flaps in first, followed by your spine flap, then your interior cover flap [C+D].

Repeat Steps 1–4 on the other cover.

Happiness indeed!

A ↓

B ↓

C ↓

D ↓

TRADITIONAL HARDCOVER BOOK

Materials ↓

- · 2 pieces of bookboard (5½ × 8½ in/140 × 216 mm)
- · 4 sheets of Judd Street 90 gsm paper trimmed to size
  - · 2 decorative sheets (7 × 10 in/178 × 254 mm)
  - · 2 interior decorative sheets (5¼ × 8¼ in/133 × 210 mm)
- · 1 length of waxed linen thread (3 yd/2.75 m)
- · 1 strip of scrap paper for your stitching template (8½ in/76 × 216 mm)

Glue the hardcovers ↓

1. Place a sheet of decorative cover paper (7 × 10 in/178 × 254 mm) decorative side down on your working surface and place one of your bookboards on top. Draw a pencil line around your cover to create your glue boundaries [A].

2. Place your cover paper decorative side down on the surface and brush the glue vertically then horizontally to smooth out any glue ridges. It's OK to glue a smidgen over the pencil lines. Position the bookboard onto the cover and press. Flip the cover over and burnish with your Teflon bone folder [B].

Note → You will notice that the paper tends to lift up a bit at the corners. If this happens use your bone folder or the palm of your hand to press – if you're using your hands be sure there's no glue on them.

3. Place the cover decorative side down again, place the corner spacer at a 45° angle and draw a pencil line. Do this on all four corners. Trim with your craft knife or scissors [C].

4. Place a piece of scrap paper under your side flaps. Swish a light layer of glue, move the glue paper aside, and use your Teflon bone folder to mould the flaps around to the back of your bookboard [D+E].

5. Place a piece of scrap paper under the top flap and brush a light swish of glue. Remove the scrap paper and crimp the nooks.

6. Use your bone folder to mould the paper around the edge of the cover and burnish with your bone folder. Repeat on the bottom flap.

Repeat Steps 1–6 to glue your second cover.

A ↓

B ↓

C ↓

D ↓

E ↓

Glue in the interior panels ↓

1. Place a piece of decorative paper (5¼ × 8¼ in/133 × 210 mm) pattern side down with a piece of scrap paper underneath. All four edges of your interior paper will be seen, so start to glue in the centre of the paper and brush off all four edges in a star pattern. Lift the glued paper and give yourself an aerial view to make sure that the edges are evenly placed, then gently rest the piece down on the inside cover and burnish with your bone folder. Repeat for the second interior cover.

2. Let your covers air dry for a few minutes, then place them under a weight to press for a couple of hours, or until flat.

Prepare your covers and signatures for stitching ↓

Note → For this style of Coptic stitch you can use an odd or even number of stations.

1. Place your six signatures between your set of covers so that the folds of the signature are facing you.

2. Jog your book on its spine and bottom edge to be sure your book is squared. Place it flat on your surface and place a book or heavy weight atop about 1 in/2.5 cm away from the spine.

3. Place your ruler flat on the surface in front of your book ½ in/13 mm from the right and position your triangle ruler up against the spine. Take your pencil and run it up along the spine against the triangle ruler, making a little mark on each of the signatures and the covers. Repeat on the left [A].

4. Decide where you'd like to place your three additional sewing stations and measure accordingly. Then use your metal ruler, triangle ruler and pencil, and follow Step 3 to mark your other sewing stations. My measurements are as on the illustration.

5. Place a piece of scrap paper (3 × 8½ in/76 × 216 mm) on your cover and align it with the spine edge. Position your triangle ruler ½ in/13 mm from the spine edge and draw a vertical pencil line.

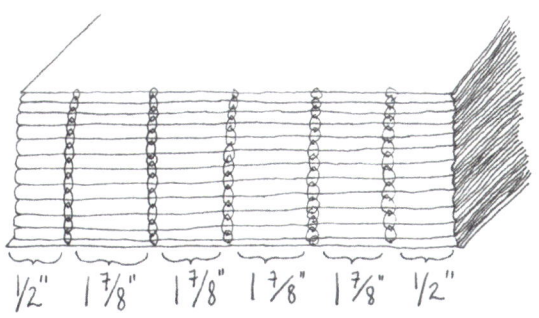

½" 1 ⅞" 1 ⅞" 1 ⅞" 1 ⅞" ½"

6. Make a pencil mark on your scrap paper at each of the sewing stations you just marked on the folds of your signature [B].

7. Align your triangle ruler with the edge of the cover horizontally. Draw a pencil line from the vertical line to the sewing station markings.

8. Place your template back on the cover and secure with washi tape. Use your medium awl to make indentations on the cover at the stations along the vertical pencil line. I prefer

to pierce from the outside to the inside of the cover [C].

9. Remove the template and finish piercing your cover [D].

Note → Be sure that your fingers are nowhere near the stations while you're piercing. I find it helpful to twist the awl back and forth until you've pushed the needle all the way through. Afterwards, take the bone folder to smooth down the protrusion.

10. Place both your covers with the fronts together and use your medium awl to make indentations through the sewing stations, as you did with your first cover, then separate the covers and pierce through the stations on your second cover [E].

A ↓

B ↓

E ↓

C ↓

D ↓

11. Position your signature stack just to the side of your surface with the folds facing you. Pick up the top signature, open it up, hold the lightweight awl in one hand and pierce through the marked sewing stations beginning at the top and making your way down. When you've completed piercing stations 1, 2 and 3, rotate your signature as if you were starting back up at the top and make your way down piercing stations 4 and 5.

12. Place the first signature with the fold facing away from you to the other side of your work surface and repeat the same steps for the remaining signatures.

Stitching ↓

Note → For this style of Coptic-stitch binding you will finish stitching your last signature simultaneously with your cover.

1. Measure the height of your book and multiply that by the number of signatures, then add 8 in/203 mm. Tie a half knot about 2 in/51 mm from the end of your thread, and thread your curved needle.

2. Position your book block slightly to the side of the centre of your workspace. Begin with your top cover and signature.

3. Exit station 1 of the signature [A]. Come round to the top of your cover to station 1 [B].

4. Pull the thread through to the right of this first stitch [C].

5. Go behind the stitch from left to right, pull gently to tighten, then enter station 1 of the signature [D+E].

6. Exit station 2. Repeat until you reach station 5.

7. Flip your book so that your first signature is facing up. Your last stitched station will now be on the left-hand side [F].

Note → Each time you bring in your next signature you will flip it to the correct orientation so your sewing stations line up, so even though you've flipped your book upside down, I will continue to refer to the station on the left as station 1.

8. Enter station 1 of your second signature [G].

A ↓

B ↓

C ↓

D ↓

9. Exit station 2, wrap around your stitch from left to right and enter station 2 [H+I].

10. Exit station 3, wrap around your stitch and enter station 3.

11. Exit station 4, wrap around your stitch and enter station 4.

12. Exit station 5, wrap around your stitch and bring in your third signature [J].

13. Enter station 5 of your third signature [K]. Exit station 4, wrap around your stitch and enter station 4 [L].

14. Exit station 3, wrap around your stitch and enter station 3.

15. Exit station 2, wrap around your stitch and enter station 2.

16. Here's where you'll make your first 'S' stitch. Exit station 1, wrap around your first stitch (cover and first signature) from left to right, and then around your second stitch (between first and second signature) from right to left. Leave a little loop. Take your needle and come through the loop, pull up and tighten. Bring in your fourth signature [M–O].

Now when you get to the end stations 1 and 5 of your next three signatures you will make an 'S' stitch and then bring in the next signature.

17. Continue stitching the remaining signatures until you complete the fifth signature. The sixth signature will be stitched in tandem with your back cover.

Note → I pull the signature out to the left a smidgen while securing the cover and then enter the signature, put the signature back into place, jog the book to straighten it, then tighten the stitch.

E ↓

F ↓

G ↓

H ↓

I ↓
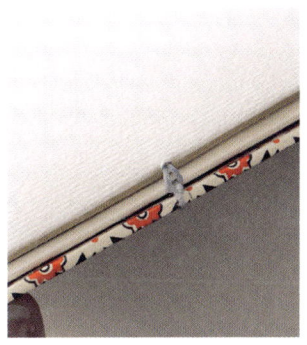

J ↓

K ↓

L ↓

M ↓

N ↓

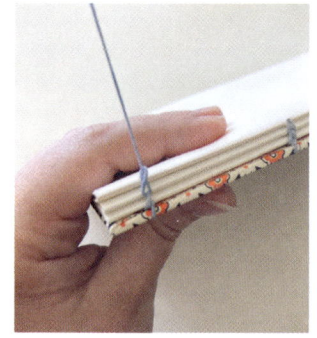

O ↓

P ↓

Q ↓

R ↓

S ↓

T ↓

U ↓

18. Place your last signature and cover on top of your book. Enter the cover at station 1 (from the top). You will continue to keep your thread length to the right of the stitch. Tighten gently with the signature in place [P].

19. Loop around that stitch from left to right, pull and tighten [Q].

20. Loop the stitch between the fourth and fifth signature (the stitch below), from left to right [R].

21. Enter station 1 of the final signature [S].

22. Exit station 2 of the signature and repeat Steps 19 and 20 at each of your stitching stations till you reach station 5 [T].

23. You will finish off inside the signature and then tie off [U].

MULTI-NEEDLE HARDCOVER BOOK

Materials ↓

- 2 pieces of bookboard (5½ × 8½ in/140 × 216 mm)
- 4 sheets of Judd Street 90 gsm paper trimmed to size
    - 2 decorative sheets (7 × 10 in/178 × 254 mm)
    - 2 interior decorative sheets (5¼ × 8¼ in/133 × 210 mm)
- 1 length of waxed linen thread (3 yd/2.75 m)
- 1 strip of scrap paper for your stitching template (8½ in/76 × 216 mm)

Glue your covers exactly as you did for the traditional hardcover book (pp.149–50).

Prepare your covers and signatures for stitching ↓

1. Place your six signatures between your set of covers so that the folds of the signatures are facing you. Follow the preparation steps for the hardcover book on pp.150–52. My measurements are as on the illustration.

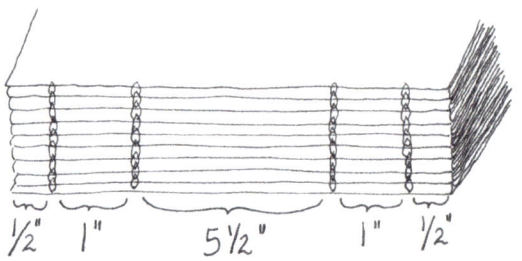

½" 1" 5½" 1" ½"

2. Place a piece of scrap paper (3 × 8½ in/76 × 216 mm) on your cover and align it with the spine edge. Position your triangle ruler ½ in/13 mm from the spine edge and draw a vertical pencil line.

3. Make a pencil mark at each of the sewing stations you just marked on the folds of your signature [A].

4. Align your triangle ruler with the edge of the cover horizontally. Draw a pencil line from the vertical line to the opposite side.

5. Place your template back on the cover and secure with washi tape. Use your medium awl to make indentations on the cover at the stations along the vertical pencil line [B].

6. Remove the template and finish piercing your cover.

7. Place both your covers with the fronts together and use your medium awl to make indentations through the sewing stations, as you did with your first cover, then separate the covers and pierce through the stations on your second cover [C].

8. Position your signature stack just to the side of your surface with the folds facing you. Pick up the top signature, open it up, hold the lightweight awl in one hand and pierce through the marked sewing stations beginning at the top and making your way down. When you've

A ↓

B ↓

C ↓

completed piercing stations 1, 2 and 3, rotate your signature as if you were starting back up at the top and make your way down, piercing stations 4 and 5.

9. Place the first signature with the fold facing away from you on the other side of your work surface and repeat the same steps for the remaining signatures.

Stitching ↓

1. Measure the distance between stations 1 and 2. Multiply that by the number of signatures and add 8 in/20 cm. You will need two identical lengths of thread. For reference, mine was 1 yard + 8in (91 + 20 cm).

2. Thread one needle onto each end of both threads [A].

3. Begin on the inside of the first signature and exit the first station with one needle, and the second station with the needle on the other end of the thread. Repeat with your

other length of thread on your other two stations [B].

4. Pull the thread through and be sure each length is divided evenly [C].

5. Begin on the left in station 1, go through the station at the top of the cover and keep your thread length to the right. Pull and tighten. Repeat for stations 2, 3 and 4 [D+E].

A ↓   B ↓   C ↓   D ↓

E ↓   F ↓   G ↓   H ↓

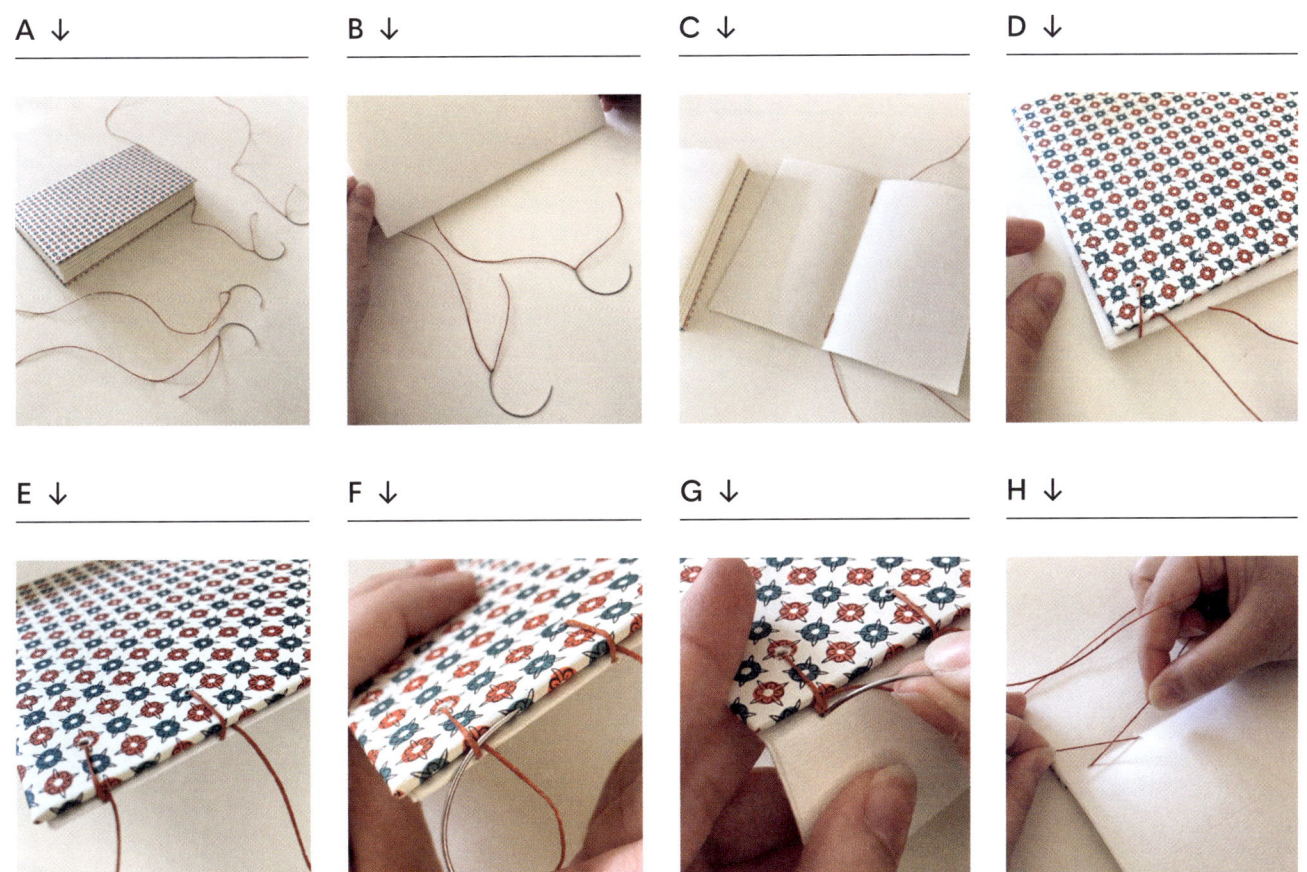

6. Take your needle from station 1 and loop around the stitch from left to right, pull and tighten. Repeat for stations 2, 3 and 4 [F].

7. Take each needle and enter the stations from 1, 2, 3 and 4 back into 1, 2, 3 and 4 – each needle returns to its original station. Now you're on the inside of the signature with all the lengths of thread [G].

8. Next you will be criss-crossing between stations 1 and 2 and 3 and 4, and then exiting the stations [H+I].

9. Now all four thread lengths will be on the outside of the signature [J].

10. Place your book cover side down with the first signature facing up and bring in your second signature. Now each needle should enter the stations directly above those on the first signature. Pull the thread lengths away from you to tighten the stitch [K].

11. Now criss-cross over stations 2 to 1 and 4 to 3 and exit the stations [L].

12. With each needle, wrap behind the stitch between the cover and the first signature [M].

13. Bring in your third signature and continue stitching in the same way, wrapping around the previous stitch [N].

14. Continue until all of your signatures are stitched in [O].

15. Bring in your cover and enter the first station of the top cover, keeping your thread to the right of the stitch. Loop behind the stitch (between the sixth signature and the cover) from left to right, pull and tighten [P].

16. Wrap your needle behind the stitch (between the fifth and sixth signatures) from right to left, then enter the sixth signature [Q].

I ↓

J ↓

K ↓

L ↓

M ↓

N ↓

O ↓

P ↓

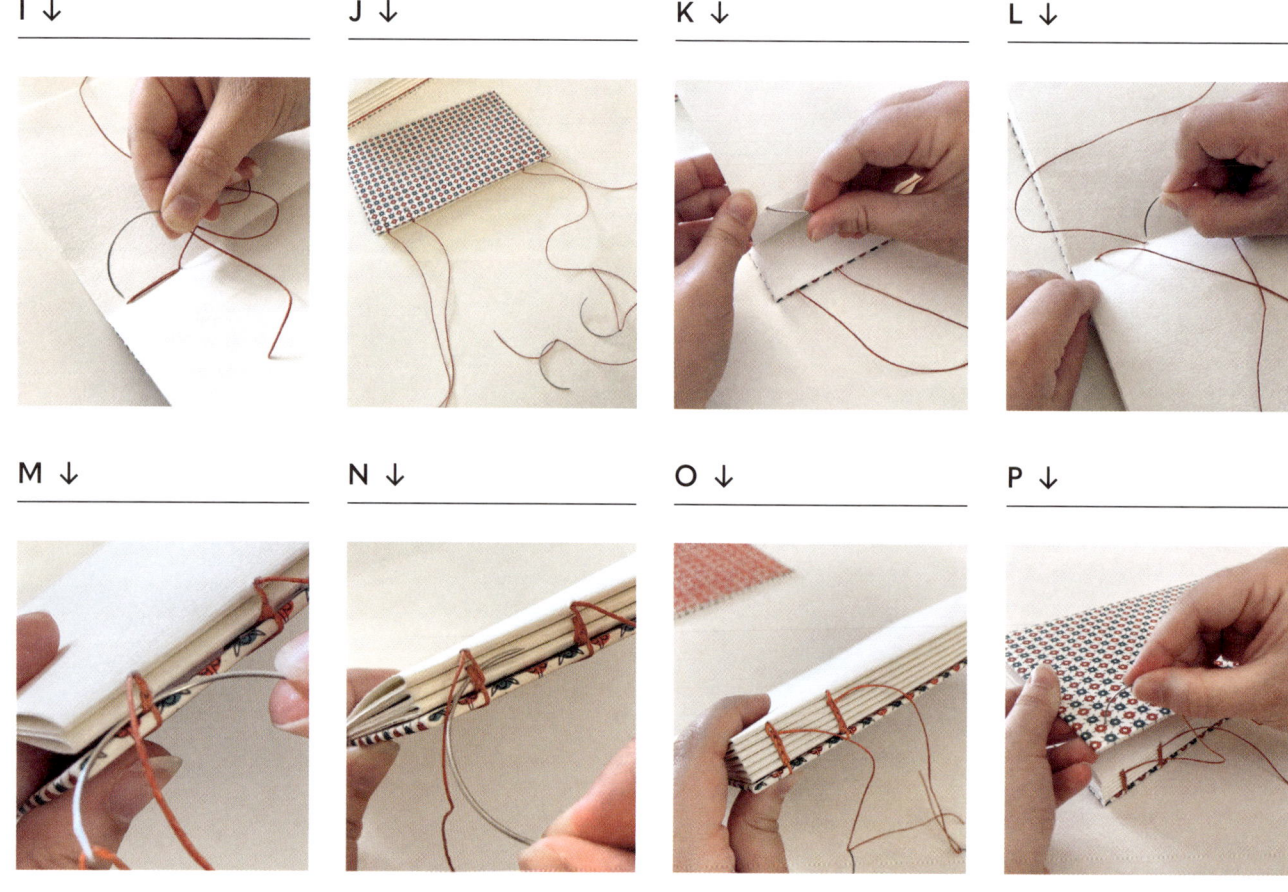

17. Once all four needles are on the inside of the sixth signature you will tie off at each station; come under the stitch, leave a little loop, pull and tighten. Then snip the threads to ¼ in/6 mm [R].

Voilà-là-là!

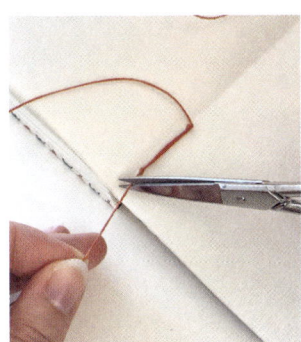

10

CASE BINDING

WHAT YOU'LL MAKE

A traditional case-bound book with hardcovers and a flat spine. The book measures 5½ × 8½ × 1⅛ in/13.9 × 21.6 × 2.8 cm with ten 8-page signatures (80 pages, 160 serendipitous sides), covered in Japanese papers and bookcloth. A swoonfully beautiful book for your doodles, poems, sketches, photos or musings.

Skill Level → ● ● ● ● ○

Materials ↓

- 2 sheets of Japanese decorative 70 gsm paper
  (6 × 10½ in/152 × 254 mm)
- 1 piece of bookcloth (2¾ × 10½ in/70 × 267 mm)
- 4 sheets of Hahnemühle Bugra (33½ × 41¾ in/851 × 1060 mm
  or 16 × 21 in/406 × 533 mm)
- 3 pieces of bookboard (0.08 point)
    - 2 pieces for the cover (5¼ × 8⅞ in/133 × 225 mm)
    - 1 piece for the spine (3 × 8⅞ in/76 × 225 mm)
- 1 length of decorative silk bookbinding headband
  (min. 2 in/51 mm)
- 1 spool of unwaxed linen thread (72 in/182 cm or width of
  your choosing)
- 2 sheets of waxed paper
    - 2 pieces for casing the book in the press
      (min. 7 × 10 in/179 × 254 mm)
    - 2 pieces for glueing in the endpapers
      (4 × 10 in/102 × 254 mm)
- 1 piece of super or Mull fabric (4 × 8¾ in/102 × 222 mm)
- 1 piece of kozo (mulberry paper) or lightweight paper
  (1 × 8¾ in/25 × 222 mm)
- 1 hinge spacer (5 × 1 in/127 × 25 mm board widths the same
  weight as your bookboard)
- 1 corner spacer (2 pieces of bookboard (1 × 5 in/254 ×
  127 mm) the same thickness as your cover, glued together)

Tools ↓

- bone folder
- Teflon bone folder
- shipping clerk's knife
- metal ruler
- triangle ruler
- lightweight awl
- size 18 bookbinding
  needle
- PVA glue
- glue brush (¾ in/19 mm)
- a cup for your glue
- scrap paper for
  glueing on
- a rag to keep your fingers
  glue free
- a wastepaper basket for
  your gluey paper
- pencil
- scissors
- cutting mat
- a small piece of beeswax
- a cloth-covered brick or
  heavy weight for pressing
- a very specific type of
  book press (see p.16)

Fold the signatures ↓

A ↓

One full-sized sheet of Hahnemühle Bugra paper (33½ × 41¾ in/851 × 1060 mm) will make four 8-page signatures. To make this case-bound book, you will fold down three full-sized sheets to make 12 signatures. You will use ten for your book and have two extra which you can use for another book, or for experimenting.

Using your full-sized sheets of Hahnemühle Bugra, follow Steps 1–3 of **Folding signatures** (see **Techniques**, p.20) three times. You now have 12 quarter sheets measuring 16¾ × 20⁶⁄₇in/425 × 529 mm.

B ↓

1. Take one quarter sheet, fold it in half with your bone folder and slice it with your shipping clerk's knife. Use your working surface to align the bottom edges, fold the two sheets together and slice with your shipping clerk's knife [A].

2. Jog the four sheets to the surface, fold gently, lining the corners up on the left, and use your bone folder to fold them into your first 8-page signature. Set it aside and carry on folding till you have a lovely stack of 12 signatures [B].

Prepare your signatures for stitching ↓

A ↓

1. Gather ten signatures and jog them to the surface on both the spine and the bottom edge. Hold the signatures firmly together and keep them aligned as best you can. Place the stack on its back with the signature folds facing you [A].

2. Before you place your heavy weight atop the book block, it's a good idea to check the alignment. I like to do that with my triangle ruler, though any straight edge will do. Place it up against the bottom of your book on the right side, then use your left hand to press the signatures into the triangle ruler. Be sure that your triangle ruler is perfectly upright. You can repeat this step along the spine edge.

B ↓

3. Gently place your heavy weight atop the book block about ½ in/13 mm away from the spine [B].

Mark the sewing stations ↓

You need six rows for your sewing stations. Use your ruler and triangle ruler in tandem for these measuring steps. Keep your heavy weight on the book block and mark your signatures following the measurements below.

1. The top and bottom stitching rows are placed ½ in/13 mm from each end. Measure and mark these end rows onto the signatures first [A].

2. Measure 1⅞ in/47 mm from the top and bottom rows towards the centre.

3. Measure 1 in/25 mm in from the last two rows, towards the centre.

4. Position your ruler flat on the surface ½ in/13 mm from the right edge of your book block and position your triangle ruler upright against the spine. Deploy your pencil and run it upwards along the triangle ruler making little pencil marks on each signature fold.

5. Repeat the ½ in/13 mm marks on the right. Then continue to mark your signatures following the illustration [B].

6. Now set the heavy weight aside, move your signatures to the side of your workspace with the folds facing you.

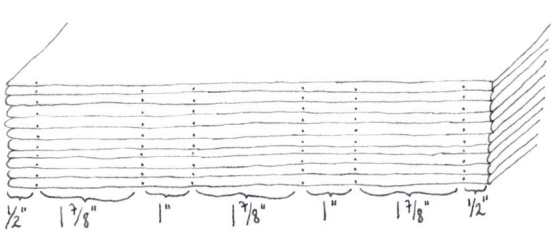

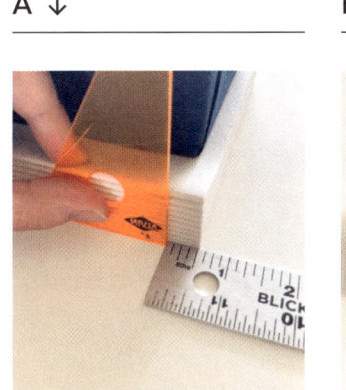

A ↓

B ↓

Pierce your signatures ↓

1. Position your signature stack just to one side with the folds facing you. Pick up the top signature, open it up, hold the lightweight awl in one hand and pierce through the marked sewing stations beginning at the top and making your way down. When you get to station 3, rotate your signature, as if you were starting back up at the top and make your way down.

2. Put the finished signature to one side with the fold facing away from you and repeat Steps 1 and 2 with the remaining signatures.

Stitch your book ↓

1. Measure your unwaxed linen thread by multiplying the height of your book by the number of signatures (ten) and adding another 6 in/15.5 cm for good measure. For reference, mine was 2½ yards/229 cm. Run the thread through a small piece of beeswax to soften the curl [A].

2. Now you will anchor the thread on your needle. Take the top tail and pull it through the eye of the needle by about 4 in/10 cm. Hold the thread between your thumb and forefinger and push the needle through the thread. Pull the thread down and onto the needle and the thread itself. Take the long thread and pull down. The knot will slide up and nestle itself close to the eye of the needle [B].

Note → When you're stitching, you might find that the thread can become unruly and curl up. I suggest dividing your thread in two, and adding the second length with a weaver's knot (see **Techniques**, p.23) If it curls while stitching you can dangle the thread and needle and let it untwist. I also run the thread through my thumb and forefinger to smooth it out. I find I need to do that after adding each signature.

3. Place your book block in front of you with the folds facing you. Then take all but the bottom signature and flip them so that the folds are facing away from you. Set them in front of you but slightly away from where you are stitching.

Note → I've numbered the sewing stations 1 to 6. 1 is at the top left and 6 is at the bottom right when the book is flat on the surface with the folds facing you.

4. Take your first signature and enter station 1 leaving a 4 in/10 cm tail of thread on the outside of your signature. Exit station 2 [C].

5. Enter station 3. Exit station 4.

6. Enter station 5. Exit station 6 [D].

7. Bring in your second signature and enter station 6. Exit station 5 [E].

8. Before entering station 4, you will first weave your thread under the stitch of your first signature, creating a cross stitch [F+G].

9. Exit station 3 and create a cross stitch before entering station 2. Then exit station 1.

10. Jog your two signatures together on the surface. Tighten the stitching if need be and then tie off with a double knot [H].

A ↓

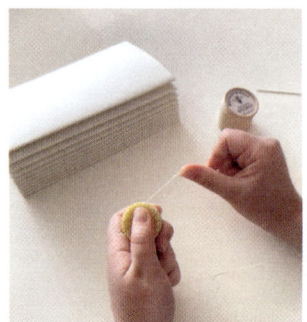

B ↓

C ↓

D ↓

11. Take your third signature and repeat the stitching from left to right, remembering to weave under the previous stitch to create your crosses. You will begin to see alternating crosses on your spine as you continue stitching [I].

12. When you reach the end of the third signature you will connect the end stations with an 'S' stitch before bringing in your next signature. You will do this at the end of each signature (on head and tail stitching rows 1 and 6) [J].

Making an 'S' stitch → This is a different 'S' stitch to the one used in the Coptic-stitch binding books.
How to make your first 'S' stitch → Run your needle from behind the previous stitch (first and second signatures), pull your thread all the way through but leave a little loop. Push your needle through the loop, pull up on your thread and tighten gently.

Note → When you stitch from station 1 to 6, your cross under will be to the left of the x. And when you stitch from stations 6 to 1, your cross under will be to the right of the x. Each time you reach the end-stitch, jog the book to the surface on the spine as well as the bottom. This helps to keep your signatures and your stitching aligned [K].

Note → It's easy to pull too tightly on this stitch which is not necessary. My first bookbinding teacher explained it well: *'If you pull your end stitch too tight, your book block will take the shape of a football.'*

13. When you finish stitching your tenth signature, your 'S' stitch will be between the eighth and ninth signature. Finish off with one more 'S' stitch between your ninth and tenth signature. Then snip the tails to ¼ in/0.5 cm or so.

E ↓

F ↓

G ↓

H ↓

I ↓

J ↓

K ↓

Prepare your spine for binding ↓

1. Jog your book block on its spine and bottom to realign the pages. Keeping it tightly formed, place it on its back on a piece of board or self-healing mat with the signature folds facing you. Use your triangle ruler (or any straight edge) to realign any shifting of the signatures. Then, place your heavy weight on the book about ¼ in/0.5 cm away from the spine.

2. Scooch the book so that the spine is very slightly hanging off the edge of the table [A].

3. Get a dab of glue on your glue brush and very lightly brush over the spine, beginning in the centre and brushing out. If you use too much glue, the spine of the book will become quite stiff and the book will not open easily [B].

4. Place the measured piece of super onto the spine and run your thumb along the super to be sure it's secure [C].

5. Brush another light layer of glue over the super and place the measured piece of kozo onto the spine. Let that dry for about half an hour [D].

A ↓

B ↓

C ↓

D ↓

Making the cover ↓

Note → The cover spine should be just a smidgen thicker than the book itself. In [A] the spine is too narrow; in [B] it is too wide. [E] shows the ideal width. I've trimmed countless spines and many times I've had to adjust after the first attempt.

A ↓

B ↓

1. Place your book flat on the surface, take your extra bookboard piece and position it vertically, flush against the spine. Make a pencil mark on your board at the top of the book [C].

2. Place the board on the cutting mat, take your triangle ruler, line it up against the base of the board, and use your craft knife to begin slicing the board. Do not try to cut the board in one swoop – it takes several glides of your knife to cut through [D].

3. After cutting your spine piece, hold it up against the book spine and squeeze it lightly. You want your spine board to measure only slightly wider than your book spine. If it's not quite right the first time, adjust and cut a second spine piece [E].

C ↓

D ↓

E ↓

Glue the cover ↓

1. First, take one of your cover boards and make a pencil mark at the top and bottom ½ in/13 mm from the edge.

2. Place your bookcloth fabric side down, lining up the pencil marks on the edge of the fabric [A].

3. Use your pencil to draw around the cover onto the bookcloth, creating your glue boundaries. Take your hinge spacer and place it snugly up against the first cover board, put your spine piece against the hinge spacer, remove the spacer and draw a pencil line around the spine piece [B].

4. Place your hinge spacer on the left of the spine, place your second cover board up against it and draw a line around the cover [C].

A ↓

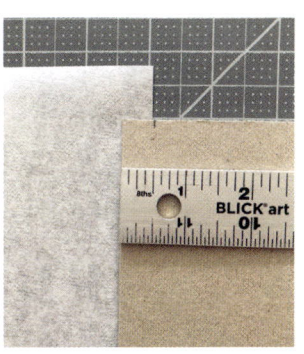

B ↓

C ↓

D ↓

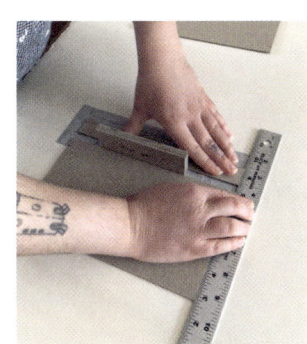

5. Place a piece of scrap paper under your bookcloth and begin glueing the area to the right of the spine, brushing your glue horizontally off the edge of the fabric. Remove the scrap paper after glueing.

6. Position your first cover piece on the glued fabric. Line up the two pencil marks with the edge of the bookcloth and press.

7. Glue your spine area, then position your hinge spacer snug up against your first cover piece and position your spine piece onto the bookcloth against the hinge spacer simultaneously and press [D].

Note → Be sure your cover and spine are aligned at the top and bottom. I often place a ruler up against the top or bottom to be sure.

8. Place a fresh piece of scrap paper under the unglued side of your bookcloth and brush on a light layer of glue. Position your hinge spacer snugly up against the spine, take your second cover piece and position it up against the hinge spacer and press. Again, be sure your covers and spines are aligned at the top. Flip your cover over onto its underside and smooth out the fabric with the bone folder [E].

9. Making sure there is no glue residue on your surface, place your cover with the bookcloth side down with a piece of scrap paper underneath it. Swish a bit of glue on your top and bottom bookcloth flaps. Remove the gluey paper away from your surface [F].

10. Use either the surface or a Teflon bone folder to mould the bookcloth around the edge of your bottom cover, and smooth out the bookcloth to the inside of the cover with your thumb and forefingers. Feel free to pinch the hinges so that they don't pucker [G].

E ↓

F ↓

G ↓

H ↓

I ↓

J ↓

K ↓

L ↓

11. Take your two Japanese decorative papers. Place the paper decorative side down, position your cover so the edge of the paper overlaps your fabric by ¼ in/13 mm, and draw around the three sides of your cover with a pencil to create your glue boundaries [H].

> Note → Here's where I like to even up the top, bottom and side flaps so that they're even all around, if necessary.

12. Place your cover face down on your surface close to where you are glueing. Take a piece of scrap paper and place it under your first piece of decorative paper and glue inside and a little over your glue boundaries [I].

13. Remove the scrap paper and lift up your glued decorative paper to give yourself an aerial view. Line it up with the edge of the bookcloth, overlapping by about ¼ in/13 mm. Once your paper is in place, press out any bubbles using your bone folder or the palm of your hand.

14. Now take your corner spacer and place it up against your top corner at a 45° angle, draw a pencil line along its edge, then use your craft knife to cut on the line. You can also cut directly along the corner spacer. Do the same for your opposite corner [J].

15. Take a piece of scrap paper, place it under your top and bottom flaps, swish a smidgen of

M ↓

glue on the flaps and then use the surface or your Teflon bone folder to mould the paper around the cover [K].

16. Now swish a light layer of glue on your fore-edge flap. Crimp in the corner nooks using the tip of your bone folder or your fingertips. This gives your corners a lovely, finished look [L].

Repeat Steps 1–16 for the back cover [M].

Measure and attach the headbands ↓

1. Place the length of headband face up on the surface. Position your bookblock so that the top of the book is nestled up against the silky portion of the headband, use your craft knife to make a nick in the headband, and then slice with your craft knife. Flip the measured piece around, line it up and measure the second piece against the original [A+B].

2. Add a dab of PVA glue and attach the headband pieces to the top of your bookblock. Be sure the bands rest snugly against the top of your signatures [C].

Case in your book ↓

Note → Be sure that your cover is dry before putting it in the press. If you've not used a case press before, I always recommend first doing a walk-through of the steps without glue to get a feel of the press and how the book rests inside.

1. Loosen the screws on the front of the press by about 3 in/7.5 cm. The back screws can be opened about the same. This is so the book can easily slide in.

2. Brush a light layer of glue in the hinge areas of the book and about 1 in/2.5 cm onto the board [A].

3. Position your book block on the spine, first giving yourself an aerial view to be sure that it is centred vertically [B].

4. Place the waxed paper sheets between the book and your super flaps on both the front and back of your book [C].

5. Lift up your book covers one at a time, keeping the book secure and pinching along the hinged area so that the fore-edges of the covers jut out evenly [D].

6. Place the book in the press, resting the hinged area of the cover along the brass edge piece.

Press the boards together and then tighten the screws gently [E].

7. Lift up the press and look at the book from all angles to be sure it's placed in the press evenly, then tighten the screws until you feel a bit of resistance. The screws do not need to be too tight [F+G].

A ↓

B ↓

C ↓

D ↓

E ↓

F ↓

G ↓

H ↓

8. Leave the book in the press for several hours, or overnight. Once the glue is dry, remove the book from the press, and remove the waxed papers from between the covers.

Glue in your end-sheets ↓

Note → Sometimes I need to trim my super flaps on the board to even them up. This is an optional step. I use a craft knife and a metal ruler and slice the super gently. Sometimes a layer of board can come up when you lift the super [H]. If that happens, just smooth it out with your Teflon bone folder. Sometimes, there might be a layer of dried glue; if that happens, you can also use your Teflon bone folder to smooth it down. Once you glue in your end-sheets it's unlikely you will see either blemishes.

Note → You might be asking yourself at this juncture, where are the end-sheets? For many moons I've been a big fan of just using the first and last pages of the book's pages as my end-sheets. At the end of this chapter I explain two ways to attach decorative end papers. The steps below explain how to glue in your end-sheets Bari Zaki Studio-style.

1. Place your book on the table with the fore-edge facing you. Raise the cover and place a sheet of scrap paper under the first page. While holding the cover up with one hand, use the other to glue your page.

2. Place a dab of glue in the centre of the page and glue off the edges on all three sides. Be sure you have a light, even amount of glue along the hinged area. Pull your scrap paper out and set that away from your work area. Let the book cover drop, then press [A+B].

3. Open the cover and place the book with the fore-edge facing away from you and the hinged area hooked on the edge of your table surface. This allows your book cover to lie flat while smoothing out your glued end-paper. Use the palm of your hand (be sure it's glue free) to smooth out the page. Run your Teflon bone folder or your thumb along the hinged area to smooth out any last bubbles [C].

4. Once you've completed smoothing out the end-paper, place a piece of waxed paper between the cover and the book block [D].

Repeat Steps 1–4 with the other end-paper.

5. After glueing in your other end-paper, place a piece of scrap paper between the waxed paper and the glued cover at both ends of the book. Place your heavy weight on your book and press for about five minutes [E].

> Note → In case you were wondering, the scrap paper absorbs the moisture from the glue.

6. Replace the scrap paper with a fresh piece and check that the hinged area is not puckering. If it is, just burnish it with your bone folder. Refresh your scrap paper again… Repeat every 15 minutes until the end-paper is mostly dry. Leave the waxed paper in and the heavy weight on for the entire time.

> Note → The best way to assess if the end-paper is dry is to check if it is cool to touch – if it is warm, it isn't dry [F]!

Leave the weight on the book overnight, with the waxed paper in place. In the morning – voilà, it's a book!

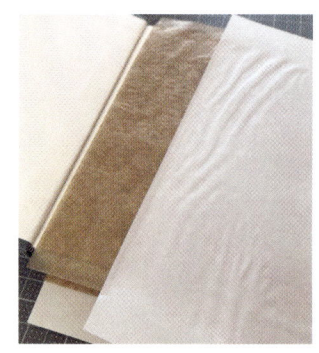

Stitching in your end-papers (optional) ↓

Before you stitch your signatures together, you will need to trim two pieces of decorative papers measuring the height and twice the width of your book block. So if you're using the Hahnemühle Bugra, it will measure (8½ × 5¼ in/22 × 13 cm). Fold them in half so that the decorative side is facing in. Place one at the top of your book block and the other at the bottom, then mark your sewing stations along with your signatures. You will stitch them as if they are signatures. And after you take the book from the bookpress, you will glue in the decorative papers exactly how I've demonstrated with my sample book.

11

BOOK OF ENGAGING PAGES

WHAT YOU'LL MAKE

An elegant book measuring 6 × 7½ × 1½ in/152 × 190 × 38 mm with four different styles of pages: six pocket pages, separated by a single-fold folio, two 4-page signatures, two three-panel gatefolded pages and two 'booklets-within-the-book', each holding a 4-page concertina. The inside covers will have envelopes/pockets at the front and back. The spine is flexible and the book lies completely flat when open.

Skill Level → ●●●●○

Materials ↓

For your cover:
- 1 sheet of Japanese Chiyogami or Katazome paper
  (11 × 18 in/179 × 457 mm)
- 1 sheet of Grafix Double Tack for your paper sandwich
  (11 × 18 in/179 × 457 mm)
- 1 sheet of Stonehenge with the grain along the short length
  (11 × 18 in/179 × 457 mm)

For your pages:
- 2 sheets of Stonehenge for reinforcing your front and
  back covers (7½ × 11 in/190 × 179 mm)
- 3 sheets of Stonehenge for your double pockets
  (11 × 12½ in/179 × 318 mm)
- 2 sheets of Stonehenge for your signatures and folios
  (22 × 30 in/559 × 672 mm)
- 2 sheets of Stonehenge for your gate folds
  (7½ × 16¼ in/190 × 413 mm)
- 2 sheets of Hahnemühle Bugra for your accordion
  (7¼ × 20 in/190 × 508 mm)

For sealing and stitching:
- 6 strips of double-adhesive tape (½ × 4 in/13 × 102 mm)
- 1 length of 4-ply waxed linen thread (4 yd/3.5 m
  should suffice)

Tools ↓

- bone folder
- shipping clerk's knife
- craft knife
- metal ruler
- triangle ruler (2 sizes)
- lightweight awl
- size 18
  bookbinding needle
- washi tape
- glue stick
- pencil
- scissors
- cutting mat
- a cloth-covered brick or
  heavy weight for pressing

Fold the signatures and gatefold ↓

Follow Steps 1–3 of **Folding signatures** (see **Techniques**, p.20) using your sheets of Stonehenge (22 × 30 in/559 × 672 mm). You now have eight pieces measuring 11 × 15 in/279 × 381 mm. You only need five of these for your signatures.

1. Take one of these pieces, fold it in half and slice again [A].

2. Fold these two sheets together creating one 4-page signature. Use the working surface to align the bottom edges, fold in half with your bone folder and set aside [B]. Repeat with the remaining four pieces.

3. Take one sheet of Stonehenge measuring 7½ × 16¼ in/190 × 413 mm. Position your page horizontally. Make your first score and fold at 5¼ in/133 mm from the right-hand side so the deckled edge is facing in after folding [C].

Note → The first step of folding your 1½ sheets of Stonehenge will provide you with a total of four 4-page signatures. When you come to organize your pages (before you stitch your book) you will then decide how many of the signatures you will divide and fold around or nestle inside any of your three 'pocket pages'.

4. Make your next score at 5½ in/140 mm to the left of your previous score, the exact width of your signature [D].

5. After these two folds you may need to trim the edge to even up the 'page'.

Repeat Steps 1–4 for your second gatefold page.

A ↓

B ↓

C ↓

D ↓

Fold the accordion ↓

1. Take your two pieces of Hahnemühle Bugra, set one aside and position the other horizontally on your working surface. Score and fold at 5 in/127 mm from the right edge of your panel [A].

A ↓

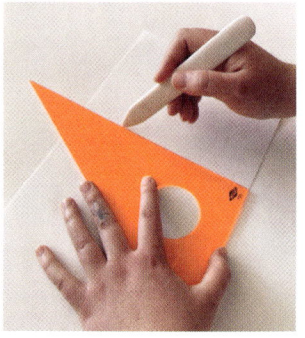

B ↓

2. Make another score line at 5 in/127 mm plus a smidgen to the left of the previous one.

3. Repeat Step 2. When you reach the end of the sheets you will have a little extra width that you can trim off with your craft knife [B].

Repeat Steps 1–3 to fold your second accordion.

Fold the pocket pages ↓

1. Position one sheet of Stonehenge (11 × 12½ in/179 × 318 mm) vertically. Deploy your bone folder, triangle ruler and metal ruler and score at 3½ in/89 mm from the right-hand side. Fold and crease with your bone folder, then open and flatten [A].

2. Rotate your sheet so the first score line is horizontal. Fold your sheet in half by lining up the corners on the left and crease with your bone folder [B].

3. Trim away the edges by ½ in/12 mm as in the illustration and photo [C].

4. Fold your side flaps inwards and crease with your bone folder. Turn your paper over and attach double-sided tape to each flap. Flip your paper back over. Expose the tape and fold the flaps in, then bring the pocket up and secure [D].

Repeat Steps 1–4 to make your two additional pocket pages.

> Note → The pocket could be a little puffy at first, but it will relax once stitched into your book.

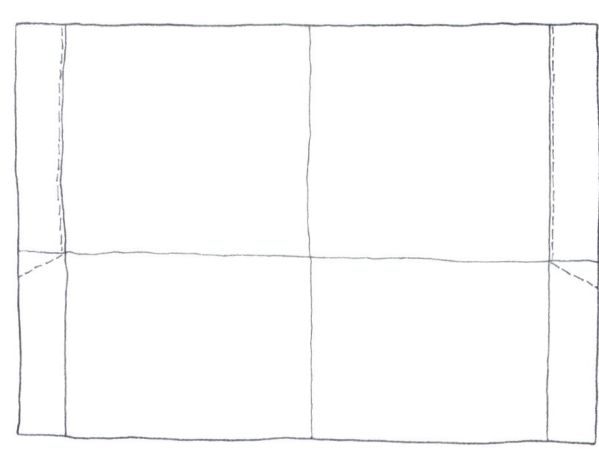

A ↓

B ↓

C ↓

D ↓

Make your cover ↓

Follow Steps 1–3 of **Making a paper sandwich** (see **Techniques**, p.21), using your sheet of Stonehenge (11 × 18 in/179 × 457 mm) as the backing paper and your Japanese paper (11 × 18 in/179 × 457 mm) as the decorative paper [A+B].

A ↓

B ↓

Prepare your cover for stitching ↓

1. Position your freshly made cover horizontally, decorative side down. Measure the width of your cover sheet. Halve that measurement and make a tiny pencil mark at the bottom of the cover at this centre point.

2. Place your book block (nine signatures and inserts) flat on the surface and place your metal ruler vertically against the folds to measure the thickness of your pages. Gently compress your signatures and release. As you 'bounce' the signatures you will find a happy medium between when the signatures are pressed down completely and when you let them puff up a bit. For reference, my spine measures 1½ in/38 mm [A].

3. Halve your spine measurement and make a second pencil mark to the right of the centre mark. This is exactly where you will make your first spine score [B].

4. Position your triangle ruler flush with the bottom of your cover and use the tip of your bone folder to score all the way from top to bottom. Give it a good crease, as you're scoring through three layers. Then fold the cover on this first score line, burnish with your bone folder, then open your cover flat [C].

5. For your second spine score, position your triangle ruler to the left of the first spine score

line, plus a smidgen. Measure at the top and bottom of your cover to be sure the triangle ruler is positioned evenly, then use your bone folder to score your second spine score line. After scoring, fold at the crease and burnish with your bone folder, then open your cover flat [D].

6. Your next score lines are the top and bottom folds of your cover. First position your cover vertically. Take one signature and place it at the spine score closest to you. Hold the cover and spine up against the signature and be sure that your signature is flush with the fold [E].

7. As you hold the signature in place, let the cover fall flat to the surface. Then, take the long end of your triangle ruler, place it up against the signature at the left, move the signature aside, then use the tip of your bone folder to score all the way from top to bottom. Fold at the score line, burnish with your bone folder then open the cover up and flatten [F].

8. Measure the height of your signature and then rotate your cover 180° so it's vertical again. Nestle your signature into the spine score and the side score, then place your triangle ruler up against the signature on the opposite side. This step is helpful to get your triangle ruler in place. Move the signature aside and add a smidgen to the measurement from the

A ↓

B ↓

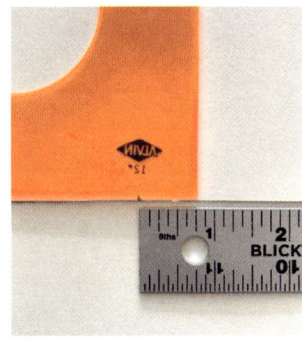

C ↓

D ↓

E ↓

F ↓

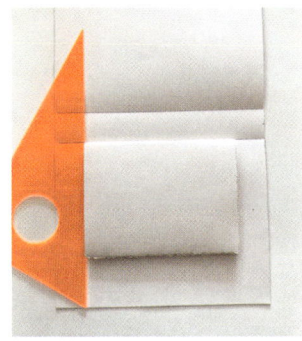

G ↓

H ↓

triangle ruler to what will be your score line. Use your bone folder to score all the way up and down. Fold over at the crease, burnish with your bone folder, and open your cover flat again [G].

9. Your next two score lines are at the fore-edge. This measurement does not have to be as precise as the previous one. I think it's nice to have a little extra room here. Measure the width of your signature and add ¼ in/6 mm to that measurement. Position your cover

horizontally and place your triangle ruler 5⅞ in/149 mm to the left of the spine score at the left. Use your ruler to confirm the distance is even at the top and the bottom. Measure, mark and score as you did with your previous score lines. Then use the tip of your bone folder to score from top to bottom (as it faces you). Fold on the score line, burnish with your bone folder, then open the cover flat, rotate your cover 180° and repeat on the other side [H].

Trim the corners and spine ↓

1. Make a pencil mark at the bottom right corner ¼ in/6 mm to the left of your vertical score line.

2. Moving clockwise, make a pencil mark 1 in/25 mm to the right of the first spine score.

3. Make a pencil mark 1 in/25 mm to the left of the spine score, and then ¼ in/6 mm to the left and right of the spine score.

4. Making your way to the top left corner, make a pencil mark ¼ in/6 mm to the right of your vertical score line.

5. Rotate your cover 90° and make a pencil mark ¼ in/6 mm to the left of that score line.

6. Continue making your way around your cover until you've marked all four corners and spine.

7. Repositioning your cover horizontally, and again starting at the bottom right corner, place your triangle ruler at the intersection of the score lines then place the tip of your craft knife into the intersection. Line your triangle ruler up with your pencil mark at the bottom edge of your cover, then slice. Make your way around the cover repeating this action on all your corners and the spine.

Prepare the spine for stitching ↓

1. Position your cover vertically and make a pencil mark ¾ in/19 mm in at the top and bottom. Then measure in 2 in/51 mm in from those two marks, creating four stitching rows.

2. Take your smaller triangle ruler, nestle it into the spine score just to the left of the first pencil mark and draw a pencil line from score line to score line. Repeat on the other side of the pencil mark. These windows are ideally ⅛ in/3 mm wide [A].

3. Nestle your triangle ruler into the spine again and use your craft knife to slice on the pencil marks you've just made [B].

Note → Don't fret too much if your first slice lands further away from the pencil mark than you'd like. You can always adjust on your second slice.

4. Use your scissors to slice the window tabs in half [C].

5. Stick down your teeny flaps with a glue stick or washi tape. Using the washi is purely for efficiency – you will not see it once you affix your reinforcing folio [D].

Note → If you use a glue stick then you'll want to press the cover under a weight for at least half an hour before continuing.

6. Trim your top and bottom spine flaps by ½ to ⅝ in/12 to 16 mm so they don't protrude into your top and bottom sewing windows. Attach a piece of double-adhesive tape to the inside of both tabs [E].

7. Take your two pieces of Stonehenge (7½ × 11 in/190 × 179 mm) and fold them in half. Trim the width slightly to 7¼ in/184 mm. Attach a strip of double-sided adhesive along the spine folds and stick them to the inside of each cover about ⅛ in/3 mm away from the spine score. Now also attach strips of adhesive to the side flaps (your fore-edge) [F].

8. Expose the adhesive on the spine tabs and side flaps, then press the spine tabs down. Fold over your top and bottom flaps, then fold over the side flap and press. Repeat on the other side [G+H].

9. Press your cover open under a weight for about half an hour to flatten before stitching.

A ↓

B ↓

C ↓

D ↓

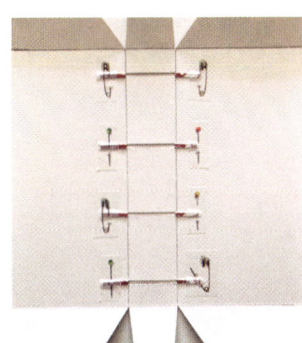

E ↓

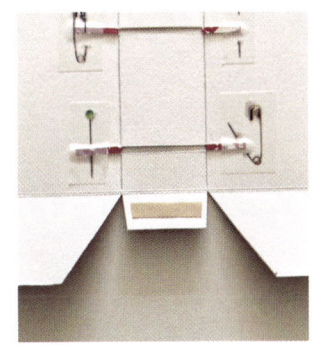

F ↓

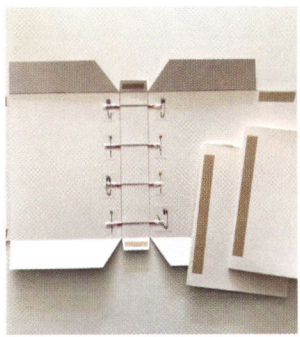

G ↓

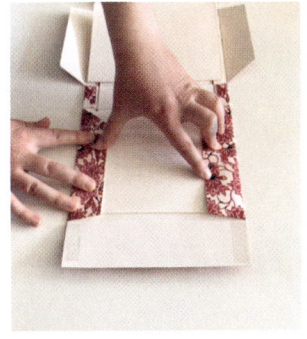

H ↓

Assemble the signatures and pockets ↓

The long-stitch binding can be stitched with an odd or even number of signatures, but the stitch is aesthetically designed for an odd number as seen in the example. The first anchor stitch (top left) is a single upright stitch, as is the last (bottom right), creating visual balance on the spine. That said, I have made numerous long-stitch books with an even number of signatures, and when you do that the two upright stitches are both at the top (or bottom) of your spine. Here are illustrations of each.

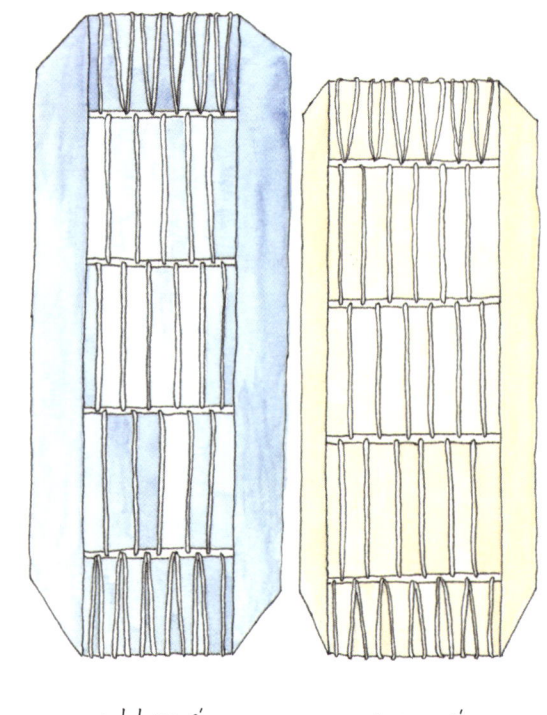

odd no. sig   even no. sig

Below is a list of how my signatures are ordered from one to nine. You can arrange yours however you'd like – there's no right or wrong way.

→ Sig 1: Full signature
→ Sig 2: Pocket with single folio
→ Sig 3: Gatefold
→ Sig 4: Full signature
→ Sig 5: Folio (with accordion)
→ Sig 6: Pocket with single folio
→ Sig 7: Gatefold
→ Sig 8: Pocket with single folio
→ Sig 9: Full signature

You will attach your Hahnemühle Bugra accordions after you've finished stitching. Suggestions for page arrangement:

→ You can divide one signature and place a single folio to the interior of your pocket page, or around it on the outside.
→ Gatefolds are a signature unto themselves.
→ Accordions can attach to a folio, or even tuck into a pocket.
→ Be sure you set one whole signature aside for reinforcing your front and back covers.
→ You can always hand-fold an envelope or two and attach them to the non-pocket pages.

Prepare your signatures for stitching ↓

1. Take your nine signatures and nestle them inside the book. Using the surface, jog them down to the spine, and then to the bottom of the book. Place your book on the surface with your spine facing you and place a light weight atop (a cloth-covered brick will be too heavy, as it just needs to keep your book stationary and not compress it) [A].

2. Take your pencil and position it exactly at the bottom centre of your stitching row. Place your triangle ruler up against the pencil tip and run the pencil up along the signatures making a dot on each of the folds. Being sure the pencil line/dots are centred. Do that at all four windows [B].

3. Remove the signatures from the cover, set your cover aside and place your signatures in front of you.

> Note → In order to keep your signatures in the order you had intended, make a light 'X' in pencil at the top right corner of each signature. This will help you keep them in order while you pierce them.

4. Position the signatures so that the folds are facing you. Take the top signature, open it up, hold the lightweight awl in one hand and pierce through the two marked sewing stations closer to the top. Then rotate the signature and pierce through the bottom two stations [C].

5. Now place your first signature with the fold facing away from you to the other side.

Repeat Steps 4 and 5 on your remaining signatures.

A ↓

B ↓

C ↓

Stitching ↓

You will begin with a length of thread six times the height of your book, and add your second length with a weaver's knot or double knot (see **Techniques**, p.23).

You will notice while stitching that the first few signatures will slide around on the spine. The signature does not get anchored in one spot to the cover, but as you continue to add your pages they will slide around less. The sewing rows are numbered 1–4 from the top to bottom, or left to right. This style of stitch begins at the back of the book, so you'll be stitching from back to front. We will begin with our ninth, final signature.

1. Measure a length of thread six times the height of your book. Thread your needle.

2. Take your ninth signature and nestle it up against the back cover. Exit station 1 through the signature and cover and leave a little tail.

3. Bring the thread up and over the top of the cover into the signature and tie off at station 1, anchoring the first signature onto the cover [A]. Exit station 2 [B].

4. Enter station 3. Exit station 4. Take your thread and bring it up around the cover and back into the signature and exit station 4 again [C+D].

5. Bring in the eighth signature. Take your thread, bring it up around the cover and into the eighth signature and exit station 4. You are now on the outside of the cover and have formed your first V-stitch [E].

6. Enter station 3. Exit station 2.

7. Enter station 1 [F].

8. Come up and around the cover and bring in your next signature. Enter station 1 of the seventh signature.

9. Go up and around the cover and enter station 1 of the seventh signature again [G]. Exit station 2.

Note → Here's where you begin to see the alternating stitching pattern.

10. Enter station 3 of the seventh signature. Exit station 4 of the seventh signature.

11. Come up and around the cover and exit station 4 of the sixth signature. Bring in the seventh signature. Take your thread, bring it up and around the cover and into the sixth signature. Exit station 4.

A ↓

B ↓

C ↓

D ↓

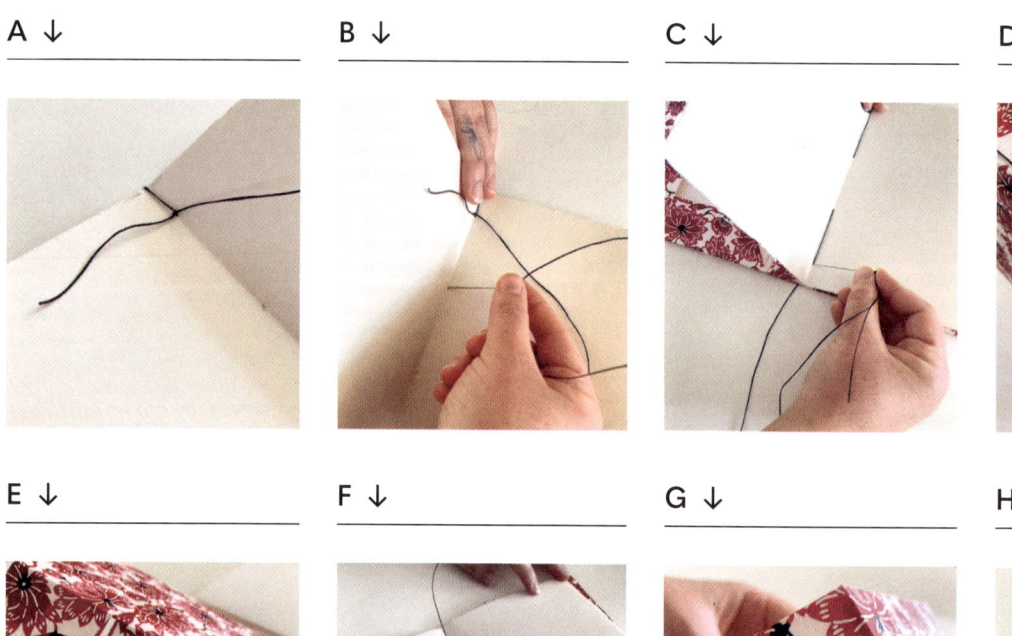

E ↓

F ↓

G ↓

H ↓

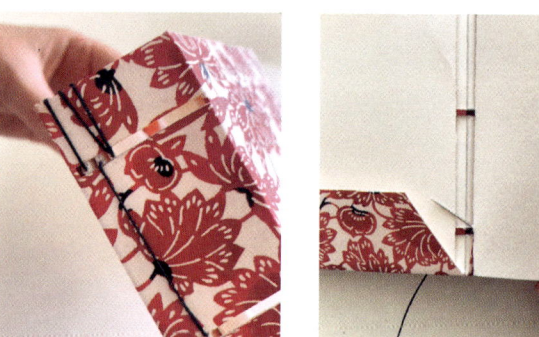

12. Enter station 3. Exit station 2.

13. Enter station 1. Come up and around the cover and bring in your fifth signature. Enter station 1.

14. Come up and around and enter station 1 of the fifth signature again.

15. Exit station 2. Enter station 3.

Note → At this point, you might begin to run out of thread and need to join your second piece with a weaver's knot (see **Techniques**, p.23). To measure the correct amount of thread for your second piece, count the number of signatures that remain and add two additional lengths the height of your cover. For example, if you have four signatures, you will need another six lengths the height of your book.

Note → The pages tend to puff up while stitching and they are easily pressed down to fit all your signatures inside the designated spine.

16. Exit station 4. Bring in the fourth signature. Go up and around and exit station 4.

17. Enter station 3. Exit station 2.

18. Enter station 1, wrap around and bring in your next signature (third).

19. Enter station 1. Exit station 2.

Repeat steps until you've reached your final signature (the first signature in your book) – your thread will be on the outside of station 4. You could tie off on the inside by bringing the thread around to the inside and simply tying a knot, though when I've finished off this way, my last anchor/V-stitch is a little loose. So, what I like to do is this for the final stitch:

20. Bring your thread around to the inside of the first signature at station 4, and exit only the signature (it helps to fold back the cover a bit) [H].

21. Enter station 3, pull and tighten then tie off [I+J].

Voilà!

I ↓

J ↓

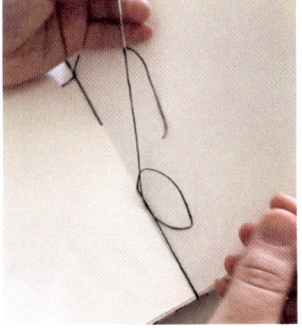

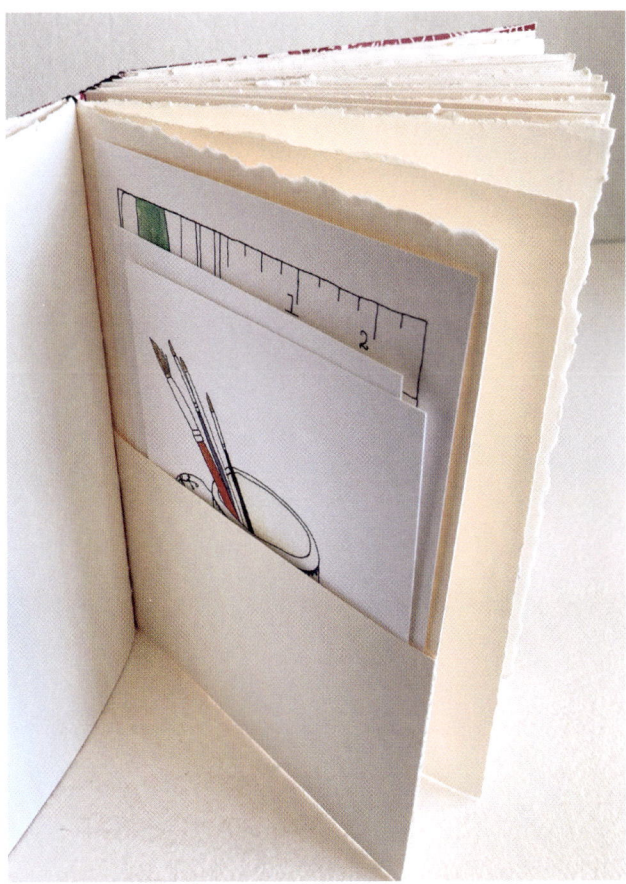

12

COLLECTOR'S ALBUM

WHAT YOU'LL MAKE

A multi-needle Coptic-stitch bound album whose 'pages' are a set of seven elegant hand-folded envelopes, perfect for organizing letters and photos, cataloguing seeds for your spring garden, or filing with ephemera and other small craft supplies. Your album will open entirely flat, so you can access the contents with ease (and delight). The finished book measures 5½ × 7½ × ¾ in/140 × 191 × 19 mm.

Materials ↓

- 2 pieces of bookboard (5½ × 7½ in/140 × 191 mm)
- 4 sheets of Wanderlust 90 gsm decorative paper for your cover
    - 2 pieces for the outer cover (7 × 9 in/178 × 229 mm)
    - 2 pieces for the interior panel (5¼ × 7¼ in/133 × 184 mm)
- 7 sheets of Hahnemühle Bugra for your paper sandwiches (10 × 13 in/254 × 330 mm)
- 7 sheets of Wanderlust 90 gsm decorative paper for your paper sandwiches (10 × 13 in/254 × 330 mm)
- 7 sheets of Grafix Double Tack (10 × 13 in/254 × 330 mm)
- 1 length of 7-ply waxed linen thread (2 yd/1.75 m)
- 7 nickel-plated paper clips (other types will be too bulky)
- 1 corner spacer (2 pieces of bookboard (1 × 5 in/254 × 127 mm) the same thickness as your cover, glued together)

Tools ↓

- bone folder
- Teflon bone folder
- craft knife
- metal ruler
- triangle ruler
- lightweight awl
- medium awl
- 2 curved needles
- PVA glue
- glue brush
- scrap paper for glueing on
- cup for your glue
- a rag to keep your fingers glue free
- washi tape
- pencil
- cutting mat
- a cloth-covered brick or heavy weight for pressing

Follow Steps 1–3 of **Making a paper sandwich** (see **Techniques**, p.21), to make seven paper sandwiches using the Hahnemühle Bugra for the backing paper and the Wanderlust sheets (10 × 13 in/254 × 330 mm) for the decorative paper [A–C].

1. Position one of your paper sandwiches horizontally. Take your ruler and triangle ruler and measure 4 in/102 mm from the right edge. Check that the distance is even at the top and bottom, and use your bone folder to score. Fold at the score line, crease with your bone folder, then open and press flat.

2. Before you make your next score line you will need to measure the height of your cover (for reference, mine was 5½ in/140 mm). Use your ruler and triangle ruler to measure that distance plus a smidgen to the left of the score line. Use your bone folder to score. This is the body of your envelope.

    ┌─────────────────────────────────────┐
    Note → After Step 2 you can determine if you are pleased with where your flap folds over onto the front of the envelope. If yes, great! If not, you can trim for a shorter flap.
    └─────────────────────────────────────┘

3. Position your paper sandwich vertically. Use your ruler and triangle ruler to measure ⅞ in/22 mm from the right side. Measure at both the top and bottom of your envelope flap to ensure that your side flap will be even, then score with your bone folder. Fold at the score line and burnish with your bone folder, then open and press flat [D].

4. Measure the width of your cover and make a note of it. You will use this measurement to finish making the body of your envelope. Use your ruler and triangle ruler in tandem to measure the distance between your first side score line and what will be your second.

Check that the space between score lines is even at the top and bottom, then score with your bone folder. Fold at the score line and burnish with your bone folder [E].

5. Trim your left flap to ⅞ in/22 mm, to match the flap on the other side [F].

A ↓

B ↓

C ↓

D ↓

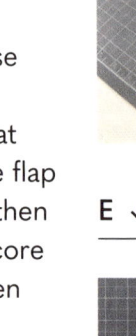

E ↓

F ↓

Trim the envelope corners ↓

> Note → In my workshops I often suggest that students make up a template from cartridge paper to practise marking and trimming their envelope, especially if it's the first time making an envelope without a template. You could also draw your trim marks directly onto your envelope.

1. Beginning at the bottom right corner, make a pencil mark ⅛ in/3 mm to the left of the score line. Make your way to the bottom left corner, make a pencil mark ⅛ in/3 mm to the right of the score line. Rotate your paper 90° and make a ⅛ in/3 mm pencil mark to the left of the score line [A].

2. You have reached the top left side flap. Make a ½ in/13 mm pencil mark to the right of the score line. Carry on making your way around the envelope with your trim marks matching the template [B].

3. Place the tip of your pencil at the intersection of the two bottom right score lines. Place your triangle ruler up against the pencil and line it up with the pencil mark at the bottom edge of your sheet, to left of the score line. Draw your trim line [C].

4. Repeat this step around the sheet until your sheet looks like this [D].

5. Slice away the corners at the pencil marks [E].

Repeat Steps 1–5 for your other six envelope pages. Keep your corners, for collage or what-have-you [F].

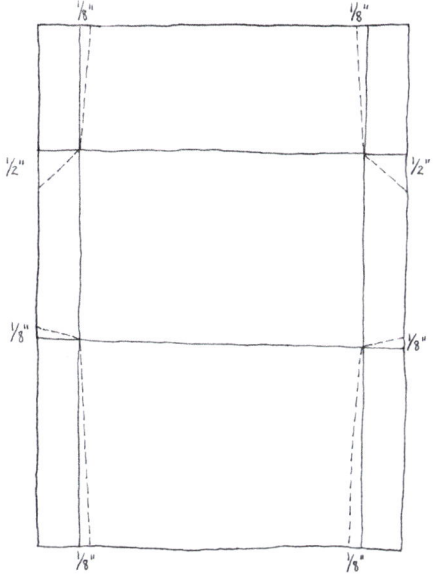

A ↓

B ↓

C ↓

D ↓

E ↓

F ↓

Glue the covers ↓

1. Place one piece of Wanderlust cover paper (7 × 9 in/178 × 229 mm) decorative side down, place your bookboard in the centre of the paper and draw a pencil line around the bookboard, creating your glue boundaries [A].

2. Keep the cover paper decorative side down on the surface. Swish a layer of glue vertically, then horizontally to smooth out any glue ridges. It's OK to glue a smidgen over the pencil lines. Position the bookboard onto the cover and press. Flip the cover over and burnish with your Teflon bone folder or your palm [B].

> Note → You will notice that the paper at the corners tends to lift up a bit. If this happens use your bone folder or the palm of your hand to press – if you're using your hands be sure there's no glue on them.

3. Place your cover decorative side down again and deploy your corner spacer. At each corner, place the corner spacer at 45° and draw a pencil line. Then trim with your craft knife or scissors [C].

> Glueing Happiness → Next you will glue down your side flaps, one at a time. Go lightly with the glue near the corners as it will only squish out when you crimp them. I prefer to use my fingernails for this part because I can feel the paper edges and corners of the boards. That said you can also use the tip of your bone folder.

4. Place a piece of scrap paper under your top and bottom flaps – as this is a landscape book, these are your long sides. Swish a light layer of glue, then move the glue paper aside and use your Teflon bone folder to lift the flaps up and mould them around your bookboard [D].

5. Place a piece of scrap paper under one of your side flaps and brush a light swish of glue [E]. Remove the scrap paper and crimp the nooks. Use your Teflon bone folder to lift up the flap and mould the paper around the edge of the cover. Burnish with your bone folder. Repeat on the opposite side flap [F].

Repeat Steps 1–5 to complete your other cover.

A ↓

B ↓

C ↓

D ↓

E ↓

F ↓

Glue in the interior panels ↓

> Note → You will want to press your covers (using a cloth-covered brick) for at least two hours before stitching. Once dry and pressed you will be ready to mark up your spine for stitching.

1. Place a piece of Wanderlust decorative paper (5¼ × 7¼ in/133 × 184 mm) decorative side down with a piece of scrap paper underneath. All four edges of your interior paper will be seen so start to glue in the centre of the paper and brush off all four edges in a star pattern.

2. Lift the glued paper to give yourself an aerial view. Be sure that the edges are evenly placed, creating a nice, even frame around the interior paper. Then gently rest the piece down on the inside cover and burnish with your bone folder.

Repeat Steps 1–2 for your second interior cover.

Prepare the covers and envelopes for stitching ↓

1. Gather your envelopes and temporarily hold the sides in place using paperclips. Organize them in your preferred order [A–C].

2. Bring in your front and back covers and jog them together, aligning them at the spine and bottom edges [D].

3. Place the album on its back with the left edge of the envelope pages facing you. Place a heavy weight atop the album about ½ in/13 mm away from the spine [E].

A ↓

B ↓

C ↓

D ↓

4. After you place your heavy weight atop of the book block, reconfirm the alignment. I like to do that with my triangle ruler, though any straight edge will do. Place it up against the bottom of your album to the right, then use your left hand to press the signatures into the triangle ruler. Be sure that your triangle ruler is perfectly upright. You can repeat this step along the spine edge [F].

E ↓

F ↓

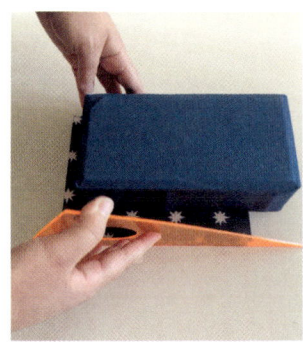

Mark your sewing stations ↓

1. Position your ruler flat on the surface 1 in/25 mm from the right edge of your book block, then position your triangle ruler upright against the spine [A].

2. Take the marker pen of your choosing and starting from the bottom of the album, run your pen upwards along the spine, making a dot on each envelope. Repeat on the left edge [B].

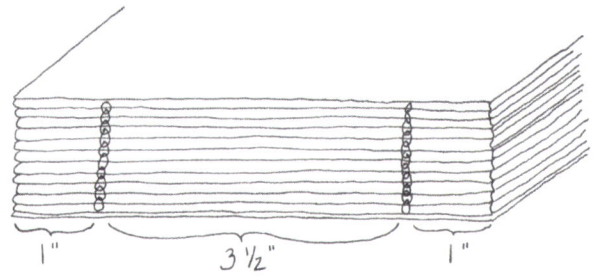

1"   3 ½"   1"

3. Set the heavy weight aside and move your envelopes to the side of your workspace with the spine side facing you.

Note → It can sometimes be a challenge to see the marked sewing stations when your pages are decorative papers. I suggest using a waterproof Japanese marker pen. A white pencil is also good, as is a Sharpie. Once you pierce through the sewing station and stitch your album, the mark will not be seen.

A ↓

B ↓

Prepare the sewing stations on the cover and pierce the sewing stations in the envelopes ↓

1. Take a piece of scrap paper (3 × 8½ in/76 × 216 mm) and use a small piece of washi tape to secure to your cover, aligned with the spine edge [A].

2. Position your triangle ruler ½ in/13 mm from the spine edge and draw a vertical pencil line [B].

3. Make a pencil mark at each of the sewing stations you just marked on the folds of your signature [C].

4. Align your triangle ruler with the edge of the cover horizontally. Draw a pencil line from the vertical line to the sewing station markings [D].

5. Use your medium awl and make an indentation on the cover at the stations along the vertical pencil line. I find it helpful to twist the awl back and forth until I've pushed it all the way through. Use the bone folder to smooth down the protrusion afterwards [E].

> Note → Be sure the fingers that are holding the cover are nowhere near the stations!

6. Remove the template and finish piercing through your cover.

7. Place both your covers together with the fronts facing and use your medium awl to make indentations through the sewing stations, as you did with your first cover, then separate the covers and pierce through the stations on your second cover [F].

8. Take the top envelope from your stack and open the side flap. Pierce both stations. Be sure your fingers are nowhere near the inside folds [G].

9. Place this first envelope with the flap facing down and do the same for the remaining envelopes.

10. Place adhesive strips on the interior bottom flaps of your envelopes. You will not seal them until you have finished stitching [H].

A ↓

B ↓

C ↓

D ↓

E ↓

F ↓

G ↓

H ↓

Stitch the album ↓

1. Attach a single paper clip to the fore-edge of each envelope (right side) to keep the flaps from flapping around while stitching. As you bring in each envelope to stitch you will remove the clip and then reattach it.

2. Measure the distance between stations 1 and 2. Multiply that by the number of signatures (seven), double it and add 8 in/20 cm for good measure. Cut a piece of thread to this length [A].

3. Thread a needle onto each end of the thread.

4. Keep your top envelope flap on the left-hand side and begin on the inside of your envelope, exiting out of both stations with each needle. Pull the thread through and be sure each length is divided evenly. Close up the envelope [B].

5. Place your cover on top. Bring your thread up to the cover entering station 1 of the cover with the needle in station 1 of the envelope. Enter station 2 of the cover with the needle in station 2. Keep your thread length to the right. Pull and tighten [C].

6. Take your needle from station 1 and loop around the stitch from left to right, pull and tighten. Repeat for station 2 [D].

7. Take your station 1 needle and re-enter station 1 of your envelope, then repeat for station 2 with the other needle. Now you're on the inside of the envelope with both lengths of thread [E].

8. Next you will criss-cross between stations 1 and 2 and exit the other station. Close up your envelope and reattach your paper clip. Your needles and thread lengths will be on the outside of the first envelope [F].

9. Turn the book so the cover is on its back and the envelope is facing up. Bring in your second

A ↓

B ↓

C ↓

D ↓

E ↓

F ↓

G ↓

H ↓

envelope and enter station 1 of envelope 2, and station 2 of envelope 2. [G]

10. Now criss-cross over stations 2 to 1 and 1 to 2 and exit the stations [H].

11. Take your needle and loop around from left to right behind the stitch between the cover and the first envelope [I].

12. Bring in your third envelope and repeat the stitching steps as you did in Steps 10 and 11, going through the stitch below each time [J].

13. Continue stitching. When you stitch on the last envelope, you will be on the outside of your album. Bring in your cover. Enter station 1 of the cover from station 1 of your envelope. Repeat for station 2 [K].

14. Bring your thread to the right of the stitch and pull to tighten [L].

15. Take your needle and wrap around the stitch from left to right between your cover and the last signature. Loop around the stitch between envelopes 6 and 7 [M+N].

16. Enter station 1 of envelope 7. Enter station 2 of envelope 7 [O].

17. Tie off inside the envelope by going under the stitch leaving a little loop, then come through the loop, pull and tighten. Snip the tail [P].

Seal the envelope flaps ↓

1. Place your album flat on the surface and open your cover. Remove the paper clip and open the bottom flap. Expose the adhesive and close the bottom flap and press. Repeat × 6!

A blush of accomplishment ensues!

I ↓

J ↓

K ↓

L ↓

M ↓

N ↓

O ↓

P ↓

GLOSSARY

Binders board →
Compressed paper board used for book covers and boxes. There are several manufacturers, so depending on each, you will see a difference with the quality. Some can be challenging to cut through without a board shear. Some cut through more easily with an X-ACTO knife.

Bookcloth →
Paper-backed fabric, specifically for glueing. Available in an enticing range of linen and silks, colours and textures.

Cloth-covered brick →
A brick covered with a piece of bookcloth. An excellent weight for pressing your book covers and keeping your signatures in place when you're marking up your sewing stations.

Cold press →
Paper with a stipple finish. Typically used for watercolour or other mediums. They are a beautiful option for book pages. You could also use them for making a softcover book. The thickest weight I find suitable for folding into book pages is 140 gsm to 250 gsm. Occasionally I will make an exception for 300 gsm.

Corner spacer →
Two small strips of bookboard glued together, the same thickness as the bookboard you are using for your project. The perfect 'tool' for measuring and trimming the corners of your decorative paper before glueing them down.

Folio →
A single piece (or sheet) of paper folded in half: a two-page signature (four serendipitous sides).

Glue boundaries →
Pencil lines drawn around your cover boards onto your bookcloth and decorative papers. Refer to my **Introduction to Glueing Happiness** chapter for a lengthier description.

Hinge spacer →
Two or five small strips of board glued together that are the same thickness as the bookboard you are using for your project. Used when you are making a hinged book cover. For example, the screw-post binder requires a two-board spacer between the covers and spine piece; the case-binding requires a five-board spacer. A suitable size for your spacer can be 1 × 5 in/2.5 × 12.7 cm. If you're making larger books, a taller hinge spacer is better.

Horizontal →
Also seen as 'widthwise'. Wider from side to side (shorter top to bottom).

Hot press →
Paper with a smooth finish, typically a paper used for watercolour or other mediums. They are a beautiful option for book pages. You could also use them for making a softcover book. The thickest weight I find suitable for folding into book pages is 140 gsm to 250 gsm. Occasionally I will make an exception for 300 gsm.

Laid finish →
If you hold a sheet of laid paper up to the light, you will notice distinct (though faint) lines, both vertical and horizontal.

Light layer of glue →
Less is more when it comes to glueing. It's better to begin light and add more if needed. Too much glue may cause issues with your materials, from too much moisture, not being able to burnish your cover materials smoothly, over buckling … or worse, glue squishing out and ending up where you don't wish it to be.

Long grain →
Grain direction that runs parallel to the long side of the sheet.

Mountain fold →
A fold in the sheet that points upwards.

Paper sandwich →
One piece of Stonehenge + one piece of double-adhesive sheet + decorative paper. An excellent (and quick) technique for making softcovers and sturdy hand-folded envelopes.

RESOURCES

Scraps →
Small bit of papers from trimming your book covers and envelopes. Great for collage bits, sharing or what-have-you.

Sewing stations →
A predetermined pierced hole (made with your lightweight awl) in the fold of your signature which allows you to easily stitch your book.

Short grain →
Grain direction that runs parallel to the short side of the sheet.

Signature (Sig.) →
Typically four sheets of paper folded in half to create an 8-page signature (16 serendipitous sides). Depending on the thickness of your paper you could increase or decrease that amount. For example, Hahnemühle Bugra at 130 gsm is perfect (in my opinion) as an 8-page signature, and the Stonehenge at 250 gsm is perfect (also in my opinion) as a 4-page signature. My exception is when making the **Chic Cambridge suite** booklets (Chapter 5), which were an 8-page signature.

Smidgen →
Close to ¹⁄₁₆ in/0.2 cm. I use this term when measuring, scoring and folding softcovers and hand-folding envelopes without a template. It's the perfect extra measurement you need to ensure the distance between your first and second corresponding score line ends up at the correct distance.

Valley fold →
A fold in the sheet that points downwards.

Vertical →
Also seen as 'lengthwise'. Shorter from side to side (wider from top to bottom)

Wove finish →
A paper with a smooth finish and no visible laid lines.

United States & Canada

Acuity Papers (Indiana, U.S.)
acuitypapers.com
Fine art papers: Awagami, Fabriano, Hahnemühle, Arches, Stonehenge.

Artist Book House (Chicago, U.S.)

Cave Paper (Arizona, U.S.)
cavepaper.com
Handmade papermakers. The fibres they use for making papers is Belgian flax, which makes an extremely strong and sturdy paper, superb for making non-adhesive style books. Although we didn't use Cave Papers in any of our chapters, we are incredibly fond of and highly recommend these papers to make any 'softcover' binding.

Colophon Book Arts Supply (Bloomington, IN, U.S.)
colophonbookarts.com
Bookcloth, threads, marbling supplies and tools.

Hiromi (California, U.S.)
hiromipaper.com
Japanese bookcloth and papers, as well as bookbinding supplies.

Hollander's (Ypsilanti, U.S.)
hollanders.com
Bookbinding supplies, tools, bookcloth, decorative papers and leather.

Hook Pottery Paper, Andrea Peterson (Indiana, U.S.)
hookpotterypaper.com
Andrea's papers are made with fibres close to home. She stocks a beautiful range of handmade papers that are very au naturel. Although we didn't use Andrea's papers in any of our chapters, we are incredibly fond of and highly recommend these papers for all manner of paper art, including glueing!

Legion Paper (New York, U.S.)

legionpaper.com

Fine art paper makers and purveyors.
The Stonehenge line is one of their signature
papers, made in the U.S. We use Stonehenge
(Cream) for the pages of our **Long-Stitch-Link-Stitch
with Hand-Folded Envelopes, Buttoned-up
Elegant Envelope Booklet, Chic Cambridge Suite,
A Trio of Concertina Techniques** and **Book of
Engaging Pages** chapters. Clearly a favourite!

Soutache (Chicago, U.S.)

soutacheribbons.com

My neighbour on Lincoln Avenue. Maili Powell is
the proprietress and button maven. She doesn't
have an online shop, but if you ever find yourself
in Chicago, I highly recommend a visit! We chose
buttons from her shop for the **Buttoned-up
Elegant Envelope Booklet** and **Long-Stitch-Link-Stitch
with Hand-Folded Envelopes** chapters.

Studio Carta, Angela Liguori (Chestnut Hill, U.S.)

studiocartashop.com

Angela exclusively imports a swoonful range of
cotton ribbons from Italy. Her range of colours,
widths and styles is breathtaking. She is the author of
The Ribbon Studio. We've stocked her ribbons in the
shop since we opened in 2015.

Talas (Brooklyn, NY, U.S.)

talasonline.com

Bookbinding tools and equipment, decorative papers,
archival materials.

Atelier Ecluse (Canada)

atelierecluse.com

100% luscious and 100% cotton handmade
paper in a beguiling selection of patterns for
covers. We used this paper in our **Buttoned-up
Elegant Envelope Booklet** chapter.

Japanese Paper Place (Toronto, Canada)

Japanesepaperplace.com

Japanese paper and paper-related products imported
from Japan since 1982 and an exceptional selection of
washi for paper-based art forms. We used their paper in
our **Case Binding, Trio of Accordion Techniques, Book
of Engaging Pages** and **Screw-post Binder** chapters.

United Kingdom

Cambridge Imprint (UK)

cambridgeimprint.co.uk

Patterned papers that are paragons of mix-and-
matchiness. The more the merrier is my motto when
it comes to CI papers. We used this paper in our
Chic Cambridge Suite chapter.

Shepherd's (London, UK)

store.bookbinding.co.uk

An enchanting shop for all manner of bookbinding
supplies and papers. We used the Judd Street
decorative papers in our **Triptych of Coptic-stitch
Bindings** chapter.

Wanderlust Papers (UK)

wanderlustpaper.co

Proprietress Lucy Brackin designs dreamy patterned
papers. We've been stocking her papers at BZS
for several years and have used them in several
workshop kits. We used her papers in our **Collector's
Album** chapter.

Europe

Carta Pura (Munich, Germany)

cartapura.de

We've been stocking all manner of Carta Pura Papers
since we opened in 2015. Need we say more? We
used their paper in our **Long-Stitch-Link-Stitch with
Hand-Folded Envelopes** chapter.

Grafiche Tassotti (Italy)

tassotti.it

Gorgeous assortment of patterned papers in a myriad
of categories. We used this paper in our **Introduction
to Glueing** chapter.

Hahnemühle (Germany)

hahnemuhle.com

We have yet to use a paper made by Hahnemühle
that we didn't love. The 'Bugra' is considered a
pastel paper but we think it is lovely for use with all
manner of mediums. It also glues beautifully. We used
Hahnemühle Bugra for the pages of our **Triptych of
Coptic-stitch Bindings** and **Case Binding** chapters.

ACKNOWLEDGEMENTS

Clare Martelli, Senior Commissioning Editor-extraordinaire. You were a beacon of light for me from the very beginning, and for that alone I am grateful beyond measure. Thank you especially for your faith in me and my work, and your continued patience and encouragement.

Natasha Collin, Editor, I am in a deep bow of gratitude to you for guiding me so easily and swiftly through the painstaking and extraordinary process of editing etc. You are an absolute delight, and I marvel at the speed at which you juggled between me, the designer, copyeditor and proofreader!

Michael Zaki (aka Zak), my beloved husband and number one fan since day one! My deepest gratitude and endless love. I would not have come this far without your unwavering encouragement, enthusiasm, support and unconditional love for me and what I do.

Ruby LaPorta, my nimble shop and studio assistant. For her steadfast reliability, musings amongst the details, hands for demonstrating the hundreds (thousands in total) of steps in each chapter. And for her technical prowess which made this book project additionally joyful bringing to life.

Janet Bouldin, dear friend, Bari Zaki Studio (BZS) in-house illustrator and whimsical watercolourist. Her beguiling way of seeing and illustrating the fine details of my bookbinding supplies and specific steps. And for her continued encouragement, support, cherished friendship, musings, lunches out and in her kitchen.

Alyson Kuhn, dear friend, postal muse, all things paper muse, longest-time collaborator, folder of exquisite envelopes and writer extraordinaire. Her way with words has brought Bari Zaki Studio to life in a way I could only dream about, but am now here.

Cat Bennett, dear friend, artist, author, Bookful co-teacher, collaborator, treasured friend and soul sister. Her continued dedication, encouragement, insight and generosity of spirit has brought light to my life and the process of writing this book.

Emery Kennett, my nimble studio and shop assistant emeritus! Her charming illustrations were the first to grace my instructional handouts when I first opened Bari Zaki Studio. She continues to visit and muse about making her next sketchbook, or stepping in to assist Ruby when I'm out of the studio.

Tammy Stams, dear friend, co-stitcher, thread winder, gluer of pencils and clips, and knitter extraordinaire. Her unwavering encouragement, humour and musings helped me get beyond the rough patches without any scratches.

My beloved and favourite Uncle Les and Aunt Sandy. For your faith in my vision of Bari Zaki Studio, and most especially for your continued support and love, always!

And my mom, who is no longer with us, but is in every little beautiful detail. She had a keen eye for exquisite materials whether she was beading, drawing, knitting or decorating. She raised my bar for aesthetics very early on.

Last but nary least, to all BZS bookbinding students. My heart is full with your continued enthusiasm and appreciation for my work and, of course, for all the questions! There are never any silly questions, they all help the learning process, and most often many other students are wondering the same thing but may not ask.